The Massey Lectures Series

The Massey Lectures are co-sponsored by Massey College, in the University of Toronto, and CBC Radio. The series was created in honour of the Right Honourable Vincent Massey, former governor general of Canada, and was inaugurated in 1961 to enable distinguished authorities to communicate the results of original study on subjects of contemporary interest.

This book comprises the 2000 Massey Lectures, "The Rights Revolution," broadcast in November 2000 as part of CBC Radio's *Ideas* series. The producer of the series was Philip Coulter; the executive producer was Richard Handler.

Michael Ignatieff

Michael Ignatieff is a Canadian-born writer and historian. His books include the trilogy *Blood and Belonging* (winner of the Lionel Gelber Award and the Gordon Montador Award), *The Warrior's Honour*, and *Virtual War*. He won the Governor General's Award for *The Russian Album*, was nominated for the Booker Prize for his novel *Scar Tissue*, and won the UBC Medal for Canadian Biography for *Isaiah Berlin: A Life*. He delivered the 2000 Tanner Lectures in Human Values at Princeton University and is currently visiting professor at the Carr Center for Human Rights Policy at Harvard's Kennedy School of Government.

ALSO BY MICHAEL IGNATIEFF

NONFICTION

A Just Measure of Pain

The Needs of Strangers

The Russian Album

Blood and Belonging: Journeys into the New Nationalism

The Warrior's Honour: Ethnic War and the Modern Conscience

Isaiah Berlin: A Life

Virtual War: Kosovo and Beyond

FICTION

Asya

Scar Tissue

The Rights Revolution

Michael Ignatieff

Anansi

6

Published in 2000 by
House of Anansi Press Limited
34 Lesmill Road
Toronto, ON M3B 2T6
Tel. (416) 445-3333
Fax (416) 445-5967
www.anansi.ca

Distributed in Canada by
General Distribution Services Inc.
325 Humber College Blvd.
Etobicoke, ON M9W 7C3
Tel. (416) 213-1919
Fax (416) 213-1917
Email cservice@genpub.com

CBC logo used by permission

04 03 02 01 00   1 2 3 4 5

CANADIAN CATALOGUING IN PUBLICATION DATA

Ignatieff, Michael
The rights revolution

(CBC Massey lectures series)
ISBN 0-88784-656-4

1. Civil Rights – Canada. 2. French language – Quebec (Province).
3. Language policy – Canada. 4. Indians of North America – Canada – Claims.
5. Indians of North America – Canada – Land tenure. I. Title II. Series.

JC599.C3I56 2000   323'.0971   C00-932546-8

Cover design: Bill Douglas @ The Bang
Typesetting: Brian Panhuyzen

Printed and bound in Canada

THE CANADA COUNCIL | LE CONSEIL DES ARTS
FOR THE ARTS | DU CANADA
SINCE 1957 | DEPUIS 1957

*We acknowledge for their financial support of our publishing program the Canada
Council for the Arts, the Ontario Arts Council, and the Government of
Canada through the Book Publishing Industry Development Program (BPIDP).*

For S. Z.

as always

Contents

PREFACE

IN THESE LECTURES I have taken three risks, and it is only fair to warn readers about them from the outset. The first is to talk about the rights revolution by talking about Canada. For non-Canadian readers, Canada is not an obviously compelling example. It is widely regarded as a boring place, decent enough but neither instructive nor interesting. This view of my native land is painful to me. I hope to prove that Canada's rights revolution is rich in implications for societies beyond its shores. In particular, I believe its experience reconciling individual and group rights within a multinational, multilingual state is actually more relevant to the circumstances of most countries than the great rights traditions of the United States, Britain, and France.

The second risk is oversimplification. These lectures, which were originally delivered to a general radio audience in Canada, are on a subject — rights — that is usually regarded as the preserve of lawyers, judges, and political theorists. And yet rights and rights talk do not belong to these worthy sages alone. They belong to us all. The trick is to say something about rights that will be meaningful to both citizens and experts. There is a danger of being condescending to the one and irritating to the other. I have tried to avoid these pitfalls, but whether I have succeeded is up to readers and listeners to decide. The lectures are intended as a modest exercise in democratic education. I hope both the book and the radio lectures will broaden and deepen the conversation of my native country and my adopted ones.

The third risk I am taking is more serious. I am writing about the rights talk of a country of which I am a citizen, but in which I have not resided since 1969. In some sense, these lectures are my attempt to catch up with the turbulent history of my country in the very years I was abroad. So it may read oddly to those who lived these years in Canada, who fought or watched the battles described in these pages. To them, this book may seem like a report by a visitor from a distant planet. I want to alert readers that I am a Martian outsider. Martians can never hope to grasp the tacit knowledge of real human beings. On the other hand, they sometimes see things real human beings fail to notice. While the rights revolution began before Pierre Trudeau came to power and continued afterwards, its course in our country was indelibly marked by his convictions and commitments. With his death, the time is right for an appraisal of his legacy.

I wrote these lectures in the Canadian Rockies, thanks to the generosity of an irreplaceable national institution, the Banff Centre for the Arts, and the Maclean Hunter Foundation. I wish to thank Carol Phillips, Don Stein, Tanis Booth, Carol Barnes, and the librarians of the Banff Centre for their warmth, humour, and efficiency. I also want to express my gratitude to the 1997–2000 graduates of the centre's program in cultural journalism, whose work did so much to reintroduce me to my native land. And I wish to thank my agent and close friend, Michael Levine, for encouraging me to write on a Canadian theme. My compromise was to choose a subject that has both a universal and a distinctively Canadian aspect. I also want to thank Robert Blitt for his rapid and accurate research. I am grateful as well to Martha Sharpe at Anansi and Philip Coulter at CBC's *Ideas* for producing the lectures, and to John Fraser and Massey College, at the University of Toronto, for providing the venue for the public lecture in the series. If the reader will pardon a final note of Martian sentiment, the exercise of writing these lectures has deepened my attachment to the place on earth that, if I needed one, I would call home.

Michael Ignatieff
September 2000

I

DEMOCRACY AND THE
RIGHTS REVOLUTION

IN THESE LECTURES, I am going to talk about a fundamental change that has come over us in our lifetime. I'm
calling this change the rights revolution, to describe the
amazing way in which rights talk has transformed how
we think about ourselves as citizens, as men and women,
and as parents. The rights revolution took off in the 1960s
in all industrialized countries, and it is still running
its course. Just think for a minute about how much rights
talk there is out there: women's rights, rights of gays and
lesbians, aboriginal rights, children's rights, language
rights, and constitutional rights. In one sense, the rights
revolution is a story of inclusion, of how previously
excluded groups obtained rights of equality. In this
regard, the extension of rights has widened and deepened
our democracy. In a second sense, however, the rights
revolution has been about protecting certain groups from
the effects of democracy. Group rights to language and
aboriginal rights to land and resources are designed to

enable minorities to protect that which is essential to their
survival from the power of elective majorities.

In other words, rights have a double-sided relationship to democracy. Rights enacted into law by
democratically elected representatives express the will of
the people. But there are also rights whose purpose is to
protect people from that will, to set limits on what
majorities can do. Human rights and constitutionally
guaranteed rights are supposed to have a special immu-
nity from restriction by the majority. This allows them to
act as a bulwark for the freedom of the vulnerable. So the
rights revolution has a double aspect: it has been about
both enhancing our right to be equal and protecting our
right to be different. Trying to do both — that is, enhancing equality while safeguarding difference — is the
essential challenge of the rights revolution, and this is
what I want to explore with you in these lectures.

Rights are something more than dry, legalistic
phrases. Because they represent our attempt to give legal
meaning to the values we care most about — dignity,
equality, and respect — rights have worked their way
deep inside our psyches. Rights are not just instruments
of the law, they are expressions of our moral identity as a
people. When we see justice done — for example, when
an unjustly imprisoned person walks free, when a person
long crushed by oppression stands up and demands her
right to be heard — we feel a deep emotion rise within us.
That emotion is the longing to live in a fair world. Rights
may be precise, legalistic, and dry, but they are the chief
means by which human beings express this longing.

It's important to understand that this longing is a global phenomenon. One of the reasons rights talk seems irresistible in Canada is that wherever we look beyond our borders, people are fighting for their rights. From 1948's Universal Declaration of Human Rights onward, the history of the past half-century has been the struggle of colonial peoples for their freedom, the struggle of minorities of colour and women for full civil rights, and the struggle of aboriginal peoples to achieve self-government. Some of these struggles are etched in my memory. I remember the television pictures of that small crowd of protesters who crossed Edmund Pettus Bridge in Selma, Alabama, on their way to Montgomery to demand the right of black people to vote in the American South. I remember the men of Attica prison, in upstate New York, who staged an uprising to protest their living conditions. The state police and national guard took the prison by force and forty-three prisoners died. Before the final assault, one of the prisoners said: "We have resolved, after long and bitter experience, that if we cannot live like men, then we are prepared to die like men."[1] From these examples, I learned that human beings value some things more than their own survival, and that rights are the language in which they commonly express the values they are willing to die for.

Struggles in Europe during the 1970s and 1980s also helped to shape Canadian awareness that the rights revolution was truly global. The campaigns by Solidarity in Poland, led by that extraordinary shipyard electrician, Lech Walesa, created the first free trade unions in the

Communist world. In Czechoslovakia, Charter 77, a movement led by writers and playwrights such as Václav Havel, demanded civil and political rights for Eastern Europeans. Finally, there were the campaigns on behalf of Soviet Jewry, in which members of the Canadian Jewish community took a prominent part. In 1990, I vividly remember travelling from Kiev, in Ukraine, to Vienna with a trainload of Soviet Jews on their way to Israel. They were frightened, bewildered, and sat up all night asking me questions about Israel, a country I had visited only once. They did not know where they were going, but they knew exactly what they were leaving: a land where even the humblest freedoms were beyond their reach. All of these battles for rights inside the Communist bloc had a huge political impact on the shape of our times. For the demand for rights was a demand to live in truth; to end the regime of lies; to live, finally, without fear and shame. What began as a campaign for rights within the Communist system ended up destroying the system altogether. When the Berlin Wall was pulled down in those unforgettable days in November 1989, the rights revolution changed history.

None of these victories came easily. The rights revolution is a story of struggle. Indeed, the concept of rights comes from the struggles of the male landholders of England and France to throw off the tyranny of barons and kings and establish rights of property and due process of law. But one of the ironies about rights is that people who win theirs don't necessarily want anyone else to have them. What dead white males fought for, they then denied to everyone who came after — women, blacks, working people. Nothing is less obvious than the idea that rights commit us to equality. Men who had enjoyed voting and property rights for centuries, for example, couldn't conceive that women should have them too, and they displayed astonishing ingenuity in denying claims that now seem self-evident. Likewise, union rights to closed shops and collective bargaining used to be regarded as a dastardly infringement on the freedom of individual workers and employers alike. This illustrates an ironic lesson: there is no more effective way to deny the rights of others than to claim that they are denying your own. The battle for union rights had to expose and defeat these claims. Workers did so by standing out in the cold in front of plant gates, and holding up placards and signs demanding the right to unionize their factories. It took from 1880 to about 1945 for North American workers to prove that collective union rights are the only effective way to counter the disproportionate economic power of employers.

History shows that there is nothing secure and unassailable about our rights heritage. At this very moment, some clever official in Ottawa, Washington, or London is devising an ingenious way to abridge our right to communicate freely on the Internet. In Britain, a Labour government — a Labour government! — is considering a bill to allow the police to monitor Internet communications. It may be a cliché, but some clichés are deeply true: the price of freedom is eternal vigilance.

Thanks to these struggles — many of them won only

in the last generation — Western liberal societies have arrived at a new moment in their history. For the first time, they are trying to make democracy work on conditions of total inclusion. Everybody has the same rights, and everybody has the right to be heard. Democracy is supposed to belong to everyone. No wonder Western elites have worried since the 1960s that our societies are becoming ungovernable. What they mean, of course, is that we citizens are less obedient, less willing to leave politics to them. The rights revolution makes society harder to control, more unruly, more contentious. This is because rights equality makes society more inclusive, and rights protection constrains government power. Countries with strongly defended rights cultures are certainly hard to govern. But who says the ways of democracy must run smooth? Democracy is rough and tumble; conflict is built into the process, but provided the conflict stops short of violence, it is better than bland or managed consensus. To paraphrase Bette Davis, fasten your seat belts, because the rights revolution makes for a bumpy ride.

Few countries have had a bumpier ride with rights than Canada. Since the 1960s, we've been in semi-permanent political crisis. While United Nations studies show that the country ranks at the very top of desirable places to live, we also rank near the top in existential anxiety about our political future. Since Quebec's Quiet Revolution in the 1960s and the more recent renaissance of the aboriginal peoples, attempts to incorporate both nations into our political fabric have brought the legitimacy of the Canadian federation into question.

Left to themselves, Canadian elites would have pre-
ferred to manage this crisis alone. What makes the
Canadian political story so interesting has been the way
in which women's organizations, aboriginal groups, and
ordinary citizens have forced their way to the table
and enlarged both the process of constitutional change and
its results. Canada has moved away from a constitutional
debate dominated by governments and first ministers to a
system of constitutional renewal driven essentially by citizens, interest groups, and nations. Constitutional change
might have begun with Prime Minister Trudeau's desire
to anchor Canadian unity in the equality of individual
rights. But by the time the process had finished, Canadians had insisted that individual rights were not enough:
guarantees for collective language rights, women's equality, multicultural heritage, and aboriginal land claims had
been forced into the Charter of Rights and Freedoms,
which was finally passed into law in 1982.

As a result, Canada has become one of the most distinctive rights cultures in the world. First, on moral
questions such as abortion, capital punishment, and gay
rights, our legal codes are notably liberal, secular, and
pro-choice. In this, they approximate European standards
more closely than American ones. Despite the fact that we
share our way of life and our public media with our
neighbours to the south, our habits of mind on rights
questions are very much our own. Second, our culture is
social democratic in its approach to rights to welfare and
public assistance. Canadians take it for granted that citizens do have the right to free health care, as well as to

unemployment insurance and publicly funded pensions. Again, the comparison with the republic to the south is noteworthy. The third distinguishing feature of our rights culture, of course, is our particular emphasis on group rights. This is expressed, first, in Quebec's Charte de la langue française (Bill 101) and, second, in the treaty agreements that have given land and resources to aboriginal groups. Apart from New Zealand, no other country has given such recognition to the idea of group rights.[2]

The fourth distinguishing feature of Canadian rights culture is that we are one of the few states that has actually put in writing, in recent Supreme Court decisions and in federal legislation, the terms and conditions for breaking our federation apart.[3] Having survived two referenda on the future of the country, Canadians rightly feared we might not survive a third. So both communities, English- and French-speaking, have sought to define the conditions under which national groups have a right to secede, how referenda on secession should be framed so that the mandate is clear, and how negotiations should take place between those departing and those remaining in the federation. Viewed from the outside, this search for "clarity" on the question of secession probably seems both crazy and dangerous. Doesn't talking about it make it more likely to happen? The Canadian gamble — or is it a strange kind of genius? — is that clarity will make breakup less likely. The idea is counterintuitive, but it is not stupid: if everybody knows the rules, nobody will be caught by surprise. Unilateral secessions are ruled out. Both sides must negotiate the terms of a divorce. If both sides understand the consequences of their actions, the chances of violence and conflict can be reduced.

The recent Supreme Court of Canada ruling on secession — now cited throughout the world as a model for any nation facing secessionist claims — understands two key ideas about rights.[4] The first is that they often conflict: Québécois rights of self-determination conflict with Canadian rights to territorial integrity, for example. The second point is that in the face of these conflicts, the purpose of rights language is to facilitate peaceful adjudication (by defining precisely what is at stake between contending parties, and in so doing to prevent conflict from turning into violence). Rights not only help to make disputes precise, and therefore manageable, but also help each party to appreciate that the other has some right on its side. The attempt to define rights of secession, in other words, is intended not to make secession easier, but to avoid the nightmare of civil war. If we do manage to avoid this nightmare, it is not because Canadians are either uniquely lucky or uniquely wise. It is because our rights culture actually works.

When viewed from the inside, Canadian politics has often seemed like a psychodrama of narrowly avoided catastrophe: referenda on secession that nearly succeeded; constitutional packages that fell apart at the last minute; standoffs between whites and aboriginals over land (and lobsters) that nearly came to blows — and sometimes did. Viewed from the outside — and this is how I have seen it, since I live and work outside my native country — Canada has been inventive in finding ways to enable a large multi-ethnic, multinational state to survive and even prosper.

Canadians may not realize it, but along with all the other things we export to the world, we also export our rights talk. It was a Canadian law professor from Montreal's McGill University, John Humphrey, who helped draft the Universal Declaration of Human Rights. Humphrey was a democratic socialist and one of the founders of the League for Social Reconstruction, which campaigned for the creation of the welfare state.[5] The Universal Declaration of Human Rights, for all its formidable abstraction, is actually an attempt to universalize Canadian social democracy as it stood in the bright dawn of victory after 1945. Many of the provisions of the declaration — including those for medical insurance, unemployment compensation, and paid holidays — may not be especially realistic as an agenda for social rights in the nations of the Third World, but they certainly encapsulate a very Canadian dream of social decency.

There are more recent examples of the central role Canadians have played in the global rights revolution. The language provisions currently being written into Baltic constitutions to guarantee the rights of the Russian minority are the work of Canadian lawyers toiling for the minority-rights commissioner of the Organization for Security and Co-operation in Europe (OSCE).[6] Another Canadian — Louise Arbour, now a judge on the Supreme Court of Canada — served as chief prosecutor for the International Criminal Tribunal for the Former Yugoslavia and the International Criminal Tribunal for

Rwanda at The Hague. It does not seem accidental that Canadians — from Arbour to General Roméo Dallaire — have been so centrally involved in the struggle to contain inter-ethnic war. As members of a multi-ethnic, multinational community, Canadians have looked with a particular premonitory horror at what happened in Yugoslavia and Rwanda.[7] For we know as well as anyone how fragile nation-states actually are, how close to violence their conflicts are, how vital it is to find justice before it is too late.

Canadians' attention to these issues has an important intellectual dimension too. Will Kymlicka, a professor at Queen's University in Kingston, Ontario, is probably the world's leading authority on group rights for minorities.[8] It is even possible to speak of a distinctively Canadian school of rights philosophy that includes Kymlicka, Charles Taylor, James Tully, Peter Russell, Stéphane Dion, and Guy Laforest.[9] These thinkers are making a theory out of the elemental experience of Canadian politics: the adjudication of rights claims between national minorities, aboriginal groups, and individuals.

The way we do this is seen, beyond our shores, as increasingly distinctive. American rights culture is intransigently individualistic, so much so that affirmative-action programs that were designed to overcome the historical disadvantages of particular groups — especially blacks and women — have run up against the belief that favouring groups in this way discriminates against individuals in other groups. And it is hard to imagine America experimenting with territorial self-government for aboriginal peoples on the scale attempted by Canada in the 1990s. The motto of the republic — *E Pluribus Unum* (Out of many, one) — hardly encourages devolution of sovereignty. In Canada, by contrast, affirmative action and aboriginal rights form an accepted part of the Charter of Rights and Freedoms.[10]

The other great global rights culture — France — has always been centralist in its vision of the French nation as a civic community of individuals united around the values of liberty, equality, and fraternity. Hence, in France, group rights claims (for example, by Muslims seeking rights to distinctive dress and religious observance) have encountered more difficulty with mainstream culture than they would have done in Canada. Britain is another example of a nation with a great rights tradition that is both strongly individualistic and strongly centralist in its essential orientation. Until recently, that is. Under pressure from the Welsh, the British Parliament has extended legal protection and state assistance to language rights, and the insistence of the Scots on their legal and cultural differences has resulted in an experiment in constitutional devolution that takes the United Kingdom some way towards a Canadian federal model.

The British, American, and French rights traditions have enormous prestige, but they have limited applicability beyond Western Europe and North America, because individualist rights regimes do not capture the dilemmas faced by societies that are both multi-ethnic and multinational (i.e., composed of founding minorities who require, as a condition of continuing membership in the state, the recognition of their rights to language, education, and self-government). These are the dilemmas for which Canadian rights talk is uniquely suited. For this reason, Canadians are found in nations from the Baltic states to Sri Lanka, preaching the virtues of group-rights regimes and federalist devolution as potential solutions to conflicts between ethnic and religious minorities inside nation-states.

Our legal culture has roots in the three great legal traditions of France, Britain, and America, and yet we do not carry the baggage of an imperial past or the menace of an imperial present. We have few enemies and many friends, and we have the problems to which the world needs answers. So it is not surprising that when the chief justice of our Supreme Court, Beverly McLachlin, visited a judicial training college during a recent trip to China, she found Chinese judges discussing Canadian Supreme Court cases.[11] When I visited the Constitutional Court of South Africa, I discovered that the judges there make frequent reference to the Canadian Charter of Rights and Freedoms.

The originality of Canadian rights culture may be obvious to South Africans, but it is not obvious to Canadians. This may reflect the woeful inadequacy of our language of identity. When we try to identify what makes us distinctive, we round up the usual suspects — everything from the winter and the land to the Mounties — but we invariably leave out our politics. Yet as outsiders familiar with our rights culture realize more readily than we do, this is the core of what makes us distinctive as a people. We are British North Americans, a colonial people in refuge from the republican experiment to the south. We are a community forged by the primal experience of negotiating terms of settlement among three peoples: the English, the French, and the aboriginal First Nations. This gives us a particular rights culture and it is this rights culture that makes us different. No matter how violently Quebecers and English Canadians disagree, they do so within political cultures that are remarkably similar. So talking about rights is a way of identifying something all Canadians have in common.

The rights revolution distinguishes us as a people, and it has changed our politics. The question is: Has it changed them for better or for worse? I've already said that the rights revolution has made our democracy more inclusive by incorporating groups and individuals who were marginalized or excluded. It hasn't even been necessary for white males like me, who have always enjoyed rights, to give up anything essential; we've merely had to find a place at the political table for newcomers. But we've also learned, sometimes painfully, a hugely important lesson: that in politics and ethics, human difference is morally irrelevant.[12] Whether someone is male or female, black or white, straight or gay may be central to their identity, but these differences should be strictly irrelevant to the way we treat them as persons. Our ideal should be that the way we treat people should depend not on who they are, but only on what they do and say. This is a new idea in history. For millennia, we've made our moral treatment of others dependent on whether they were female or male, black or white, abled or disabled, young or old. Only in very recent history have we begun to try to live by an ideal of equality that ignores these differences and treats people as individual members of the same human race.

Let me illustrate this point by telling you about my mother's idea of utopia. She always used to say that utopia is not a place where you love everybody — it is a place where when you hate somebody, you hate him for good reason (i.e., because he has done bad things). So her utopia was a place where both love and hate were strictly personal. To my way of thinking, my mother made the best case there can be for a certain kind of moral individualism, one that insists that the important differences in human conduct are individual, not group or collective ones. It is character, not skin colour, and conduct, not identity, that matters when we size people up.

The question is not whether we believe in this — because we do — but what we actually do to make it come about. We need to look more closely, with a little less self-congratulation, at the gulf between what the rights revolution has promised and what it has actually delivered. Just ask aboriginal peoples. They've had their treaty rights acknowledged at long last. But does that make life better on Native lands than it was fifty years ago? Has the aboriginal renaissance in our country cut into the suicide rate among teenagers on Northern Ontario reserves? Hardly. Nobody would claim that having these rights has made matters worse. But nobody is confident that it has made things much better.

Rights talk may even have become a substitute for reform. More intellectual and moral attention has been given to treaty rights and aboriginal self-government than to the often appalling social conditions on reserves. Aboriginal rights doctrine grows more subtle, and the elites — the professors, policy-makers, and aboriginal politicians who have mastered this doctrine — are making a good living out of rights talk. But are things getting better in Davis Inlet and Burnt Church? To the people in these communities, rights talk remains just talk. Cynics observing this process might almost suspect that elites talk not in order to make things happen, but so that they can sustain the illusion that things are changing for the better.

It's not even clear that everybody is getting more rights. Some people are losing theirs. Ask organized labour, for example. They'd say they have fewer rights — and less power — than they had fifty years ago. Closed-shop agreements have been challenged, successfully, on the grounds that they violate the right of the individual to choose what group he wishes to join. Even if we grant that individual and collective rights in the labour market need always to be balanced, it is clear that the pendulum has swung too far. Too many workers have no job security, no pension rights, no holiday rights, and they are working too many hours. This is the dark side of our affluence. It's not true that everyone has benefited or benefited equally from the rights revolution.

The problem is not just the gap between rhetoric and performance; there's a problem with the rhetoric itself. Is it a good thing that rights talk has become the primary language of contemporary politics? What happens when disputes between Canadians — the stuff of politics — become conflicts of rights? In the old days, if you will pardon a generalization, politics was about interests. Interests can always be traded, but rights cannot. We've got too much invested in them for that. We think of them as trumps. "Give me my rights" is not an invitation to compromise. It's a demand for unconditional surrender.

When a claim is turned into a right, it doesn't necessarily make it easier to settle. It may, in fact, make it harder. Some people say politics has got a lot shriller since rights talk took it over. It has made our personal life shriller too. The Personal Is Political was a notable feminist slogan. But when personal behaviour is politicized, when rights enter the bedroom, moral absolutism sometimes takes over. In the other lectures in this book, I'll be looking closely at what happened when the rights revolution entered our private lives.

I'll also be looking at a related question: Does rights talk bring us together or drive us apart? Pierre Trudeau believed the Charter of Rights and Freedoms would bring us together. Yet the results haven't worked out that way. Many of the Supreme Court's rulings on Charter appeals have been divisive. Some people think Charter rights of free speech are being abused by Holocaust deniers; other people think that rights to due process of law are being exploited by male defendants in rape cases.[13] More broadly, the rights revolution sometimes seems to have fragmented the political community into aggrieved victims' groups, each seeking its rights at the expense of the others: women against men, aboriginal peoples against non-aboriginals, children versus parents, Anglo-Canadians versus Québécois, and so on.

Rights talk may be dividing us because of how it enfranchises and recognizes groups. Group rights are supposed to be necessary to protect those essential things — such as land and language — that can't be protected unless a group is guaranteed the right to have them.

But where are such rights leading us? The problem is not merely that collective rights pit groups against groups; they also pit individuals against groups. Almost everybody thinks that aboriginals should have the right to strengthen their self-government, but what happens if individuals don't want to take part? Should their rights prevail over those of the group? If so, the very future of the group may be jeopardized. Or take an example from Orthodox Judaism. It's a good thing to give groups the right to practise their religion, of course, but is it so good if the women can't take part in the prayers? If a woman rebels at this subordination and wants to leave, does the group have the right to compel her to stay? Can it force her out if she tries to change the practices of the group? Many of our toughest choices involve reconciling our belief that groups should have the right to protect their identities from outside pressures with our equal belief that they shouldn't oppress the individuals inside them.[14] One of the later lectures in this book tries to reconcile group rights with individual freedom.

On the face of it, reconciling these conflicts ought to be

easy. Groups should be able to protect their cultures and practices against the intrusions of the majority, but they should not be able to deny their individual members rights of protest and rights of exit. So far so good. The problem is that many groups — aboriginal peoples, religious communities, and so on — don't see themselves as communities of rights-bearing equals. They think group purposes should prevail over freedom of choice. This is certainly the case with the Muslim and Orthodox Jewish communities in our midst. They say that if a society protects individual rights of protest and exit, it will end up destroying the group.[15] In the end, we will have to choose between individual and group rights, and I hope to show, in a later lecture, why we should allow individual rights to prevail.

Another issue running through these lectures is whether rights talk has actually reduced inequality. Certainly some civil inequalities between men and women, between gays and straights, between Québécois and English Canadians, have been addressed by rights talk. But what about inequalities between rich and poor? One of the strange features of rights talk has been that it makes visible some inequalities — sexual and linguistic inequalities, for example — while obscuring others — such as those based on class and income. I'm no Marxist, but I am astonished that social and economic inequality, the focus of so much socialist passion when I was a student, has simply disappeared from the political agenda in Canada and most other capitalist societies. This disappearance has something to do with rights talk. It can capture civil and political inequalities, but it can't capture more basic economic inequalities, such as the ways in which the economy rewards owners and investors at the expense of workers. The economic system may not infringe anybody's individual rights, but the whole machine ends up reproducing enduring types of social inequality. Rights talk not only fails to capture this kind of inequality, but also diverts the attention of the political system from it.[16] So in the past thirty years, we've talked about women, aboriginals, gays, and lesbians. But what about the workers? What about the way their union rights have been eroded? What about the economic insecurity of our poorest fellow citizens? Why can't our politics address this? It can't be because everyone has shared the fruits of our recent economic boom. It can't be because the poor don't exist. It must be because they have become invisible. Is this the fault of the way rights talk dominates our political language?

These lectures are not intended to offer a wholehearted endorsement of either rights talk or the rights revolution. I also want to highlight the limitations of rights talk as a language of politics. It's not just that rights talk has a way of throwing light on some injustices while consigning others to political darkness. It's also that rights talk ends up monopolizing our language of the good. One way to see this is to think about the family. These lectures will devote more space than political philosophy usually does to the impact of rights on family and intimate life. Much of this impact has been positive. It's obviously a good thing for children to have rights (for there to be limits on the kind of corporal punishment that can be inflicted, for example).[17] It's very important that women have the same rights as men to matrimonial assets and equal rights in divorce. In some sense, all of these changes aim at recreating the family in the image of a community of rights-bearing equals. But it sounds cold and heartless to think of a family in those terms. Rights talk doesn't begin to capture the web of love and trust that makes real families work.

Trying to capture these values in the language of rights only makes for confusion. It doesn't make any sense to talk about kids enjoying a right to love. A right to fair and equal treatment, sure; protection from abuse, certainly. But love isn't a juridical thing at all. It's not an enforceable duty or even an obligation.

We should beware of the ways in which rights talk can swallow up the whole of our language of what is good in private and public life. And we should realize that protecting the rights of individuals within a family isn't enough to keep our family life healthy. Never before have individuals had so many rights within family life. Never have divorce rates been higher.

Some critics go a step further and actually attribute the long-standing crisis in our family life to the rights revolution. If there wasn't so much loose talk about rights, so the argument goes, and there was more talk about responsibilities, we wouldn't have families falling apart at such high rates. Sometimes, the target of this indignation is feminism, and sometimes it widens out to attack the very idea of rights itself. This indignation is trying to express the real anguish many people feel about family life today, but it's got the problem upside down. No one seriously supposes that we're going to make family life better by taking away women's rights and the rights of children. The challenge is to make an enduring institution out of a community of equals. Giving everyone rights clearly isn't enough, but it can help. If men know they can't get their way by smacking women and children around, then they have to start talking. In other words, rights can help us make the turn towards deliberation, towards negotiating rather than fighting. Rights can also address inequalities in the division of labour. Women leave marriages because the institution becomes unequal, unfair, and loveless all at once. Providing more rights for women and more state-sponsored child care and other aids, may — I say may — make the division less unfair. As for children, rights laws aren't there to turn families into communes or Polish parliaments where everyone has a veto. They're there to stop beatings, terror, intimidation, and violence.

This leads to a more general point. Rights are not a language of the good at all. They're just a language of the right.[18] Codes of rights cannot be expected to define what the good life is, what love and faithfulness and honour are. Codes of rights are about defining the minimum conditions for any life at all. So in the case of the family they are about defining the negatives: abuse and violence. Rights can't define the positives: love, forbearance, humour, charity, endurance. We need other words to do that, and we need to make sure that rights talk doesn't end up crowding out all the other ways we express our deepest and most enduring needs.

A still more general point ensues. Rights regimes exist not to define how lives should be led, but to define the condition for any kind of life at all, the basic freedoms necessary to the enjoyment of any kind of agency. Agency is the key idea in rights. The word "agency" just means the capacity of individuals to set themselves goals and accomplish them as they see fit. The basic intuition of rights talk is that if individuals have agency, if they have the capacity to act in the world with some degree of freedom, they can protect themselves and those they love from abuse, and they can define for themselves the type of life they want to live.

To say that rights are about protecting agency is to say that rights are about protecting individuals.[19] Now individualism has a bad name. But since life is often a matter of choosing between evils rather than goods, I prefer the evils of capitalist individualism to the evils of collectivism. Historically speaking, coercive communities have done more harm. We've run three serious experiments in the twentieth century to create communities that would replace narrow capitalist selfishness with communitarian fervour — experiments by Hitler, Stalin, and Mao — and the results are definitive.

My point is not that communities always end up in tyranny. In democratic societies, neighbourhoods and community associations often succeed in reconciling collective belonging with individual autonomy. But that is the test of whether they are successful. Communities are valuable to the degree that they articulate individual goals and aspirations, to the degree that they allow individuals to accomplish goals they could not accomplish alone. Group rights — to language, culture, religious expression, and land — are valuable to the degree that they enhance the freedom of individuals. This suggests that when group rights and individual rights conflict, individual rights should prevail. The basic intuition of rights talk is that each of us is an end in ourselves, not a means to an end. This is because each of us wishes to frame our own purposes and achieve them in so far as we can. These purposes are valuable to us because they are expressive as well as instrumental. When we achieve them, we express our identities as well as serve our interests. That's why agency is so valuable to us. I don't think this individualism is Western or time-bound. It's just a fact about us as a species: we frame purposes individually, in ways that other creatures do not.

So when you engage in rights talk, you are committed to a certain kind of individualism. This has its limits. I've mentioned the difficulty rights talk has in focusing the social and economic inequality that accompanies the competitive individualism of market society. Doing something serious about inequality means infringing on property rights. We hesitate to take this step not just because large capitalists have political power, but also because most of us are property holders ourselves, and we use our power in the political marketplace to resist the taxation necessary to make a redistributive dent in inequality. The problem, in short, is neither individualism nor individual rights. Nor is it capitalism. The chief obstacle to making a dent in inequality is democracy.

If rights can't be blamed for inequality, they can't be blamed for disuniting the country either. Modern societies are conflictual: class against class, interest against interest, men against women, workers against employers. In this, Marx was deeply right. Rights are there to help adjudicate these conflicts, and these adjudications are never final. The longing for finality is a reactionary delusion, as is the longing for national unity, consensus, and a quiet life. Rights bring conflicts out into the open. But there are ways in which they also help us to resolve them. First, rights talk can show opposing groups that there is right on the other side. In this way, people's understanding of what is at stake in a conflict slowly changes. Instead of a battle between right and wrong, the conflict begins to be seen as a battle between competing rights. At first, this may only reinforce self-righteousness. But after a while, when one side realizes that the other has a rights claim too, compromise can become possible. Rights talk clarifies disagreements and creates the common language in which agreement can eventually be found.

Rights consciousness also creates the grounds for understanding what kind of community we are, and in so doing helps us to keep the show on the road (i.e., binds us together as a people and as a country). For the key ideas of rights talk are that we are all deliberative equals, that each of us has a right to be heard about the public business of our country, that no one's claims can be silenced and denied simply by the fact of who they are. This ideal

of deliberative equality — the commitment to remain in
the same room talking until we resolve our disputes, and
to do so without violence — is as much unity, as much
community, as modern life can afford.[20] The key point
here is that rights talk, by creating this idea of deliberative
equality, has widened the democratic conversation of
societies like ours. I grew up in a Canada where the conversation of the country was firmly in the hands of a
political and economic elite. Since the 1960s, the rights
revolution has brought to the table whole new groups
that were never heard before, and the debate about what
kind of society this should be has become noisier, less
controllable, and more democratic than it was before. For
this, we have to thank the rights revolution.

II

HUMAN RIGHTS AND
HUMAN DIFFERENCES

IN THE LAST LECTURE, I described how the rights revolution has changed our country in the past thirty years —
that is, how new groups have fought to establish their
rights, and why our political culture (with its emphasis
on group rights to both language and land) has made us a
more distinctive people than we realize.

But we're getting ahead of ourselves. We've plunged
into the middle of the subject, and in so doing we've
missed some important issues. Why do we have rights in
the first place? What exactly does it mean to have a right?

If we ask these questions in our own country, the
answers seem obvious. Citizens have rights because our
ancestors fought for them. Rights are not privileges given
by those who rule us — we've either inherited them from
past struggles or won them with our own two hands.
When people found governments, they do so not in a
state of nature, as Jean-Jacques Rousseau supposed, but
in historical time, and they come to the business of

making new rules of government with pre-existing rights. This was the case with the American colonists who declared their independence in 1776. Their Declaration of Independence was not an attempt to create rights out of nothing, but an affirmation that their existing rights as British colonists had been abused and a proclamation that thenceforward they would safeguard those rights in a constitution of their own. The British North Americans who created Canada in 1867 had rights prior to our act of confederation simply by virtue of being British citizens in crown colonies. So too did aboriginal peoples. They were self-governing nations, and their rights of self-government were confirmed by the British Proclamation of 1763. As we know, these rights were not originally recognized, and it's taken Canada and the United States more than 120 years to correct that injustice.

Constitutions do not create our rights; they recognize and codify the ones we already have, and provide means for their protection. We already possess our rights in two senses: either because our ancestors secured them or because they are inherent in the very idea of being human. Such inherent rights would include the right not to be tortured, abused, beaten, or starved. These inherent rights we now call human rights, and they have force whether or not they are explicitly recognized in the laws of nation-states. Thus human rights may be violated even when no state law is being infringed.

This idea that rights are prior to government, either because they are historically acquired or because they are inherent in being human, is meant to set limits on what government authorities can do to us. Legislatures and governments do not give us our rights; they are there to respect the rights we possess already. This takes us to a third sense of the word "prior": governments and legislatures exist to protect, defend, and where we deem necessary, extend our rights. Rights define not only the limits of government power, but also its very purpose.

If we have a grievance that involves a violation of our rights, then the proper authorities must investigate and act. In this sense, rights are about giving grievances legitimacy. Once they have legitimacy, then redress is supposed to ensue. Not all grievances get legitimacy, of course. For example, nobody's rights are being infringed when the heads of corporations earn a hundred times more than their employees. Gross income inequalities in our society may be wrong, but they are not illegal. Thus rights give salience to some wrongs while remaining silent about others. Some people think this makes rights useless. Others believe it turns rights regimes into an apology for capitalism. I don't agree. It just means that some grievances can't be fixed by the courts; they have to be fixed by politics, and in our system, a grievance that doesn't convince a majority of our fellow citizens, however just it may be, doesn't get fixed. As I said in my last lecture, democracy is one reason why inequalities of income have proven so hard to contain. Most Canadians are unwilling to lend their support to serious measures of redistribution. Indeed, such measures are seen as infringements on the rights of individuals.[1]

For this reason, rights talk tends to focus attention not

on the way the private economy runs, but on the way power is exercised over us by state authorities. Rights have both a positive and a negative relationship to state power. Positively, rights define our entitlements to state programs, such as unemployment insurance, welfare, health care, and pensions. Negatively, rights are the instrument we have to rein in what Shakespeare called the insolence of office. Our rights are supposed to prevent governments from reading our mail, taking away our property without compensation, or making decisions without our consent. Not everybody is happy with the way rights restrain governments.[2] Social democrats think that property rights have had a negative impact, since they prevent government from redistributing income and resources; conservatives feel precisely the opposite — that rights should be there to protect us from government's good intentions. It's no use complaining that rights talk fails to end these political arguments about what is just. Rights are there to help us determine what is right, not necessarily what is just. Establishing what is just involves balancing rights claims, which is to imply that rights conflict: my right to property versus yours, your right to privacy versus the public's right to know, and so on.

Nor is it the function of rights to promote a particular political philosophy. It is beside the point to say, for example, that recent rights decisions by our Supreme Court aren't progressive enough. Rights aren't intrinsically in the service of either progressive causes or conservative ones. They're just there to keep our arguments orderly.

Rights make explicit the rival claims that must be adjudicated if a society is to be just. And to the degree that rights are procedural — the right to due process of law, for example — they also lay down the rules societies need to observe to prevent rights conflicts from turning violent.

Yet rights are more than a set of procedures. They're not neutral. They express commitments, such as avoiding violence and treating people equally. Because they express values, they're not just the rules of an unchanging status quo. Values can be turned against the system whenever it fails to deliver. And no system of law ever fully lives up to its ideals. The right to vote and the right to due process of law express a commitment to human equality that we preach better than we practise. Black people in the American South took these promises seriously, even though they lived in a society that betrayed them every day. They marched against the arrayed power of the police and sat on the steps of courthouses not just to secure these rights, but to find recognition for their equality as human beings. So rights are never just instrumental. They aren't valuable just because they allow people to protect themselves or advance their interests. They are valuable because their possession is a crucial recognition of their moral worth.

Rights are also there to help us resolve our conflicts with our fellow citizens. These rights give us entitlements, but they also simultaneously exercise a constraint: we're not allowed to solve our disputes by force or fraud. Rights commit us to deliberating together, to agreeing to adjudication when we cannot find a compromise ourselves, and to abstaining from violence if we don't get our own way. This teaches us that every right entails an obligation. My right to go about my business without being assaulted or abused goes with an equal obligation to avoid doing the same to others. The reciprocal character of rights is what makes them social. It is what makes it possible for rights to create community.

I don't want to sound pious or naïve; I'm describing the way our society ought to work, not the way it actually does. Nobody, least of all me, supposes that rights have driven force and violence from our society. We are a long way from the ideal — but the ideal is not powerless either. And the ideal is that we try to live in a shared world based on right rather than might. The ideal is not there to lull us into sleep; it's a continual reminder to rulers and ruled alike that we do not actually live by what we say we believe.

The wider point to make is that rights never securely legitimize the status quo; they actually make grievance legitimate, and in so doing compel societies to continue their partial, inadequate, and therefore unending process of reform. This idea that society is forever incomplete, forever in search of a justice that remains beyond its grasp, is characteristic of modern societies everywhere. Ancient empires — the Aztecs, the Moguls, the Chinese — thought of themselves as finished creations, works of art that could not be superseded or improved. People in modern societies cannot think in this way. One reason is our rights talk. It condemns modern societies to a permanent self-inquisition, a permanent self-questioning. It is largely because of rights, therefore, that, in the Polish philosopher Leszek Kolakowski's words, modernity is on endless trial.[3]

The claim that rights just make us selfish individual-ists, defending ourselves against all comers, hardly captures the truth of the matter. First of all, some rights, such as those protecting freedom of assembly and free-dom of speech, were expressly created to enable individuals to get together and create communities of belief, faith, and commitment. Without these rights there wouldn't have been, for example, any socialist or union politics in this country. Second, having rights means respecting the rights of others. Respect doesn't have to mean sympathy, friendship, or fellow feeling. We can function with far less. Respect actually means listening to something you'd rather not hear, and listening must include the possibility of recognizing that there may be right on the other side.

Rights alone cannot create community feeling — you need a common history and shared experience for that. But living in a rights culture can deepen one component of community, which is trust. It's not full, loving trust of the kind you get in good families or happy marriages. A rights culture is properly poised between faith and suspi-cion: we trust each other just enough to argue out our differences, but not so much as to forget the possibility that others may be tempted to tread upon our rights.

So rights do more than legitimize individual griev-ances. They express values, and in so doing help foster conditional respect and a limited kind of community. It is the very nature of this community that everyone in it will have moments of disillusion, fears about the fragility of the fabric that holds it together. For a rights community is in constant dispute. The balance it seeks is just enough collective sense of purpose to resolve these disputes, but not so much as to force individuals into a communitarian strait-jacket.

So far I have been talking about civil and political rights, and the kind of political community — disputatious, unfinished, and yet coherent — they help to create. These rights derive from citizenship in particular national communities. It is the relationship of rights to remedies provided by these nations that gives them a clear meaning. Now I want to shift the focus to another category: human rights. These are the inherent ones I referred to earlier, the ones that derive from the simple fact of being human. They don't derive from citizenship or membership in a particular nation. So where do we get them from? And how do we enforce them? Here we are in a murky place. Imagine asking someone who he is, only to have him reply, "I'm a human being." That's not much of an answer. If he replies, "I am a Canadian," however, you know who you are talking to. The basic problem with the idea of human rights is that it is not clear what community the rights refer to, or what actual remedies they confer.

Of course, someone will immediately reply that the community to which human rights refers is the human race. But what kind of community is that? Moreover, what kind of identity is it? As a matter of fact, we never encounter human beings as such in our daily lives, only as determinate members of particular races, classes, professions, tribes, religions, or communities. When they present themselves to us, and we to them, difference is the focus: particular names, places of birth or origin, individual beliefs and commitments. Human differences are what define us, not the humanity we share.

The problem of what kind of identity our human identity actually is has bothered thinkers for a long time. The French Revolutionaries sought to universalize the idea of human rights in the Declaration of the Rights of Man and Citizen in 1791. Writing some years after the French Revolution, the wise old reactionary Joseph de Maistre remarked that he'd met a lot of people in his life — Frenchmen, Spaniards, and Portuguese; men and women; rich and poor — but that he'd never actually met a Man, with a capital *M*.[4]

The British philosopher Jeremy Bentham, writing in the same era, said much the same. What we call human rights he called nonsense on stilts, meaning that he just couldn't see whose rights these were exactly, and how they were supposed to be enforced.[5] And if you can't enforce a right, what's the point of having it?

If all human beings were safely ensconced within political communities that accorded them basic rights, then Bentham and Maistre's point would be conclusive. In reality, rights-respecting societies are a rare, even endangered, species. In the real world, billions of human beings live in despotic regimes, or in collapsed or failed states where nothing is secure. They need human rights because those are the only rights they have. This helps us to see human rights as a residual system of entitlement that people have irrespective of citizenship, irrespective of the states in which they happen to find themselves. Human rights are the rights men and women have when all else fails them.

If all else has failed them, they have no remedies, and they must look to their own defence. Human rights express the principle that when the governed are oppressed beyond hope of remedy, they have a right to defend themselves. This justifies the most radical step human beings can ever embark upon: taking the law into their own hands.

Taking the law into one's own hands doesn't just, or even necessarily, mean taking up arms. It may mean appealing for help beyond one's own borders. Human rights create extraterritorial relationships between people who can't protect themselves and people who have the resources to assist them. The rights revolution since 1945 has widened the bounds of community so that our obligations no longer cease at our own frontiers. This new culture of obligation, when coupled with the emergence of global media bringing us pictures of the anguish and suffering of strangers beyond our borders,[6] presents us with old moral dilemmas in a new form: Who is my brother? Who is my sister? Whose needs must I make my own? Whose rights, besides my own, must I defend?

These questions arise in relation to not only strangers far away, but also those much closer to home, as close as the holding pens of our international airports: emigrants, refugees, or asylum-seekers. They have some rights under our system, but they remain vulnerable to administrative and police abuse, and so it's important that they have human rights protection. Their chief protection is the UN's 1951 convention on asylum. It mandates that people in one country have a right to be accepted in another if they can demonstrate a well-founded fear of persecution. If they can prove this, they can't be sent back to face arrest or abuse. To be sure, these rights are abused by economic migrants, but it is the nature of rights to be abused. Abuse doesn't justify the abrogation of the right for all, merely its more effective policing against abuse by some.

It is legitimate to make the right of asylum conditional on the stipulation that the persons must be in danger — just as it is legitimate for communities to limit the number of immigrants they take in every year.[7] Too much immigration too fast can overwhelm the capacity of societies to treat people fairly and help them make a new start. Too little immigration turns rich societies into exclusive and unequal clubs. Immigration policy struggles to reconcile commitments to people in danger and in need with equal commitments to safeguard a national community's cohesiveness and capacity to care.[8]

Human rights are there to protect people who do not have secure citizenship, or who arrive at our doors without rights of their own. Human rights are also important to those who have secure citizenship rights. Even democratic states with strong legal institutions and rights traditions can and do abuse the human rights of their citizens. They can do so with perfect legality, as the conditions of many of the prisons in Western societies make plain. No law is actually broken when a prisoner is kept in solitary confinement for excessive periods of time, or when he is treated with contempt by prison guards. Yet his human rights are violated by these acts. The justification for this legal but unjust treatment is that those who commit crimes forfeit the right to be treated with decency. This is a simple mistake — the penalties of the law prescribe only the loss of certain rights, not the loss of all — but it is a mistake deeply anchored in retributive instinct, and hundreds of years of rights traditions have done little to correct it in the minds of the public. The idea of human rights incarnates the contrary proposition: that no matter what a person has done, he cannot forfeit his right to decent treatment.

Western societies have done a poor job living up to this injunction. It should be a matter of shame, for example, that from the late 1930s to the 1970s, thousands of people were forcibly sterilized and sometimes even lobotomized in state institutions for the mentally handicapped in this country and many others. It was all done in their best interests, of course, by doctors who told themselves the dangerous fable that their intentions were above all possible reproach. In Alberta and several other Canadian and American jurisdictions, as well as in Scandinavia, young women who were labelled "sub-normal," and therefore deemed incapable of responsible parenting, were sterilized without their consent on the basis of eugenics legislation passed with the enthusiastic endorsement of the medical community.[9]

One of the essential functions of human-rights legislation is to protect human beings from the therapeutic good intentions of others. It does so by mandating an obligation to respect human agency — however expressed, however limited — and to desist from any actions, even those that are intended to help, if these agents refuse or in any other way give signs of a contrary will. (For to be human is to have a will, however constrained, limited, or fallible.) To be sure, keeping to this rule is hard, but the test of human respect always lies with the hard cases — the babbling, incontinent inhabitant of a psychiatric ward or a nursing home; the prisoner who has shown no respect for others and now asks for respect from us; the uncontrollable adolescent whose behaviour seems to cry out for coercive restraint. To give these human beings the benefit of informed consent, the rule of law, and such autonomy as they can exercise without harm to others is the proof that we actually believe in human rights.

Yet human rights alone are not enough. In extreme situations, we need extra resources, especially humour, compassion, and self-control. These virtues in turn must draw on a deep sense of human indivisibility, a recognition of us in them and them in us, that rights doctrines express but in themselves have no power to instil in the human heart.

In this sense, that old reactionary, Joseph de Maistre, was wrong. We have met Man. He is us. Human rights derive their force in our conscience from this sense that we belong to one species, and that we recognize ourselves in every single human being we meet. So to recognize and respect a stranger is to recognize and respect ourselves. As paradoxical as it may sound, having an intense sense of one's own worth is a precondition for recognizing the worth of others.

On the other hand, recognizing other people as human is not easy. Sometimes the humans in question may be violent, gross, abusive, crazy, or just so plain different in language, values, and culture that it is genuinely hard to see what we do have in common.

Let us also admit that there is nothing especially natural about this kind of human recognition, about the feeling that the human species is one. Historically speaking, this idea, the work of monotheistic religions and natural law, is a rather recent addition to the moral vocabulary of humankind. This universalism has had to make its way into our hearts against a much more intuitively obvious notion: that the only people we should care about are people like us.

In *Bleak House*, Charles Dickens left us an immortal satire of the good philanthropic lady of mid-nineteenth-century England, Mrs. Jellyby, who never stopped campaigning for the welfare of children in Africa. Her face had the faraway look of someone always focused on distant wrongs. Dickens's problem with this charitable lady, of course, was that she shamefully neglected her own children.[10] We all know people who combine high-flown commitment to human rights with lowdown disregard for all the actual human beings who stand in their way. It seems obvious that charity, not to mention decency, begins at home, and that we have good reason to put our primary moral emphasis on particular duties to those nearest us.

Yet our commitments are connected — ever-widening circles that begin with those who are close to us and move outwards to embrace the needs of strangers. Human-rights commitments are on the outermost arc of our obligations, but they can be only as strong as our inner-most commitments. Believing fiercely in the value of those we love is the very condition for believing in the value of those farthest away. Universal beliefs that do not draw their fire from the passion for particular people are not going to stay alight for long.

To say this is to commit ourselves to a special way of thinking about the relationship between human equality and human difference. In this way of thinking, human equality actually manifests itself in our differences. What we have in common as human beings is the very way we differentiate ourselves — as peoples, as communities, and as individuals. So it is not the naked body we share in common, but the astoundingly different ways in which we decorate, adorn, perfume, and costume our bodies in order to proclaim our identities as men, women, mem-bers of this tribe or that community.[11]

To be forced to strip naked before a cold-eyed stranger is a terrible experience. Human beings clothed, arrayed, disguised even, are the ones who have dignity, not human beings stripped and bare, hiding their shame with their hands. To be naked before a stranger is to be deprived of decency and also of agency. Of course, nakedness can awaken pity, and this is a very basic form of human recognition, but it is also the most vulnerable form, for it implies the weakness and fragility of one party. We know from historical experience that when persons depend for their lives on the pity of others, they are uniquely defenceless.

In the destruction of European Jewry in the Holocaust, one of the essential techniques of dehumanization was to strip everyone of their possessions, their clothing, their glasses, even their hair. A concentration camp could be seen as a demonic machine whose purpose was to take historical individuals in all their particularity and pound them on the anvil of suffering into pure units of humanity. When these pure units of humanity then appealed to the pity of their captors, they discovered that their captors regarded them as so much meat. When those responsible for this crime had reduced each individual to the terrible equality of nakedness, they could do anything to their victims that they wished. In such a state of equal and radical humiliation, victims would even go unresistingly to their own deaths.

Not all went unresistingly, of course, and those who survived best were those who held on, against all the odds, to such fragments of personality, faith, humour, or intransigence that distinguished them from the horrible equality of all the others. This is not to say that this tenacious insistence on difference alienated them from the rest. Rather, it was by holding on to their individuality that people pulverized by suffering could acknowledge others, care for them, and resist together as best they could.[12]

The function of human rights, then, is not to protect the abstract human identity of nakedness, or to express in juridical language our instincts of pity for denuded human suffering. Its function is to protect real men and women in all their history, language, and culture, in all their incorrigible and irreducible difference. The purpose of human rights is not to make those in danger the wards of conscience of those in zones of safety, but to protect, defend, and restore the agency of the defenceless so that they can defend themselves.[13]

Human rights are not just for those who have lost all other rights. They also serve a vital function for those who live in developed civil- and political-rights regimes. Since Roman times, the European tradition has developed an idea of natural law, whose purpose is to provide an ideal vantage point from which to criticize and revise actually existing law. There has always been a deep tension between those who take the law as it is — rough and ready, precedent-driven — and those who want the law to be the ideal conclusion of a single rational mind. Natural law arose from a desire to bring order to the jungle of law, and to remedy its injustice by reference to a universal standard. Natural law has provided a vantage point from which to criticize laws as they were, and to uphold a right of resistance when they could not be changed.[14]

Our idea of human rights descends from this tradition of natural law. In the contemporary world, human rights have provided an international standard of best practice that has been used to upgrade and improve our civil and political rights. So in Europe, for example, when citizens of Britain have a grievance and their laws provide no remedy, they can take their case to the European Court of Human Rights in Strasbourg. Often, this court will find against British law, and when it does, the British usually, though not always, revise their statutes accordingly.[15]

Let's not suppose that the British are always happy about this procedure, however. Many believe it to be an affront to national sovereignty. What right do "they" — meaning the judges of Strasbourg — have to alter national laws?

This takes us into an important issue of principle. Many people feel that any such override by an international body interferes with the rights of national cultures to define their own laws. In Britain, the override has legitimacy because the European Convention on Human Rights draws on legal traditions that the British recognize as similar to their own. But in many countries in the Islamic world, in Africa and Asia, human-rights movements are seen as an alien attempt to impose European standards on cultures and norms that have their own legitimacy.

What entitles Westerners to enforce human rights on other cultures? Nothing does. If rights are about protecting human agency, then they require us to respect the way other human beings use their agency. The argument that people in other cultures would adopt human-rights standards if they only knew what we know — and that therefore we can intervene, whether or not they want us to — is simply wrong. The idea that some people are unable to discern their own real interests is an invariable alibi of paternalism or tyranny. Victims are victims only if they say they are. The corollary is also true: we're mandated to intervene on their behalf only if other peoples and cultures ask for help.

Rights language mandates respect, and respect mandates consent. If in Pakistan — or Canada, for that matter — women consent to remain within Islamic law, that is their business. If, on the other hand, they seek an education or want to marry someone of their own choosing, and they ask for our help against religious or secular authorities, then we can step in to aid them as best we can. But help means help; it doesn't mean conversion or assimilation. We've got no business inflicting our way of life upon them. Rights talk and Western culture are quite separable. Other cultures want to have rights protection without choosing Western dress, food, or technology. To the degree that Westerners are drawn into assisting other cultures, they are under an obligation, one intrinsic to rights language itself, to respect the autonomy of the cultures in which they work.

This problem of reconciling human-rights standards with local values doesn't occur only in non-Western societies. It also occurs close to home. In Western societies, law is supposed to be the expression of popular sovereignty. Hence in our societies, as in non-Western ones, a real question arises: Should human-rights codes, drafted as they are by a bunch of international lawyers who are elected by nobody, have precedence over national laws passed by representatives of the people?

One of the places where they ask this question is the

United States. The U.S. Congress has repeatedly refused to ratify international human-rights documents, from the genocide convention to the Geneva Convention's additional protocols and the Convention on the Rights of the Child.[16] Congress construes these documents as either inconsistent with American law or an intrusion on the sovereignty of Congress and the American people. Behind this attitude lies what might be called rights narcissism, the idea that the land of the free and home of the brave has nothing to learn from anybody else.[17] So America has a paradoxical relationship to human rights: its own constitution embodies a noble rights tradition, and American leaders such as Eleanor Roosevelt have helped write international human-rights texts,[18] but Congress and large sectors of the American people believe that nobody outside their country has any business criticizing the conditions of their prisons or the possibly biased, unjust, and unfair way that capital punishment is carried out in certain states, especially Texas.

Human rights, therefore, are in conflict with popular sovereignty as an expression of national culture.[19] But this conflict is a necessary one. Democracies are not always right. When majority decisions are unjust, dissenting minorities must have the capacity to appeal to a higher law. Human-rights legislation provides just such a language of appeal. In the United States, those who oppose capital punishment do so in the name of both the U.S. constitution and international human rights. There is no way to eliminate the tension between human-rights principles and democracy. Indeed, the tension is essential to the preservation of liberty.

In Canada, governments do not always respect our civil and political rights. They may even suspend them sometimes, as happened with the War Measures Act in October 1970, when the federal government, believing there was a civil insurrection in Quebec, used military power to arrest more than 500 individuals suspected of terrorist sympathies and hold them without trial. When the emergency passed, basic rights were restored. But what if they aren't? What if governments take them away for good? These things happen. Germany of the 1920s was a democracy, with a constitution and the rule of law. But the Great Depression and the ensuing economic chaos drove millions of German voters into the arms of Hitler. It cannot be repeated too often that when Hitler came to power in 1933, he enjoyed vast popular support. So did the reforms he subsequently put through: abolishing the rights of certain citizens to marry, acquire property, and vote. These Nuremberg Laws, which abrogated the rights of citizens who happened to be Jewish, were enforced by lawyers and judges raised in the best traditions of European law. One terrifying aspect of Nazi Germany is how gross and immoral injustice was given the semblance of legality, and how these injustices basked in popular support. Indeed, had Hitler died in 1937, he might have gone to his grave as the most esteemed German since Goethe. The lesson of this story is that even a Reichtstadt, even a lawful society, can lend its support to measures that turn fellow citizens into pariahs. From the denial of civic rights to the obligation to wear a yellow star in public was but one step. And from the yellow star to deportation to the east was but another. And with deportation to the east, as far as most Germans were concerned, the problem simply disappeared.

This terrible story tells us that there must be some higher law, some set of rights that no government, no human authority, can take away. The purpose of this higher law is to rouse the individual conscience from its slumber. When that happens, perhaps an ordinary citizen, watching his neighbours being taken away, will have the courage to think, This may be legal, but it is not right. Then he or she may say, out loud, "This must stop. Now."

Such moral courage is always a mystery, but we know that it springs from example, from what our mothers and fathers taught us was right, and also from what our culture tells us we should believe. The cultural resources of the German people were immense: from Schiller's "Ode to Joy," which celebrates the deep oneness of all mankind, to Beethoven's "Fidelio," with its unforgettable ode to freedom. Yet we know that these great works did not inspire ordinary Germans to see the abomination that was before their very eyes.

In the face of the insufficiency of Europe's existing cultural resources, the Allies were determined to create a new language capable of strengthening the capacity of ordinary people to refuse unjust orders and to stand up when fellow human beings were taken away. The central idea was indivisibility — that is, that no one's rights are separate from anyone else's, and that if they come in the night to violate the rights of Jews, they are violating the rights of everyone. This is the deeper context, I think, in which we should understand the emergence of human rights after the Second World War. The Universal Declaration of Human Rights, proclaimed by the United Nations in December 1948, was the first of a spreading canopy of laws whose essential function was to give ordinary human beings the capacity to recognize evil when they see it, as well as the authority to denounce and oppose it. Human-rights legislation is thus one instrument we have devised to strengthen civic courage and deepen the capacity of individuals to stand up for each other.

The Universal Declaration of Human Rights altered the balance between national sovereignty and individual rights. With the declaration, the rights of individuals were supposed to prevail over the rights of states when those states engaged in abominable practices. This might be the most revolutionary of all the changes that have taken place since the peace of Westphalia established the European order of states in 1648. With each passing year, we get closer to a new dispensation in which the sovereign rights of states are conditional upon there being adequate protections for the basic human rights of citizens. Where states consistently abuse human rights, where all peaceful remedies have been exhausted, the UN may authorize intervention, from sanctions all the way up to a full-scale military campaign. From the world of the 1930s, where the violations of the German Reich were viewed as a strictly internal matter, to the world of the 1990s, where violations in a province of Serbia end up justifying military intervention, we have travelled a long way.

Yet many people increasingly question the destination to which human rights seem to be headed. The emerging obligation to protect strangers outside our own borders is indeterminate and unclear — and it could also be dangerous. It may be a warrant for imperialism, and imperialism contradicts one of the basic rights we have: to rule ourselves free of outside interference.

The interventions of the 1990s — Somalia, Bosnia, Kosovo — were all justified in the name of human rights, and all involved a potential conflict with the right of peoples to live their lives without interference. How are we to resolve this conflict? Our obligation to care for the human rights of others is limited by rights talk itself. We have no business intervening in other people's lives unless they explicitly ask for help. The basic rules that apply overseas also apply at home. You may have next-door neighbours who fight. You can hear their arguments through the party wall. You don't have any right to intervene. It's their business. But if you hear a blow, a cry, and a call for help, you'd be something less than a citizen, and possibly something less than a human being, if you didn't come through the door to break up the dispute.

Those who criticize interventions in the name of human rights on the grounds that we must always respect the sovereignty of a state need to remember that the victims of that state are usually imploring us to intervene. That's the first condition that must be met if interventions are justified: victims must be demanding our help. Other conditions follow: the abuses must be gross and systematic; they must be spilling over into other countries, causing refugee flows and instability in nearby states; and intervention must stand a genuine chance of stopping the abuses. Intervention has no justification as punishment; its only purpose is to protect. Another condition is that intervention must be a last resort. Force is never just unless all other peaceful means of finding a solution have been exhausted. Those who intervene must also seek the consent of the international community, preferably the UN's Security Council. We don't want a world in which human-rights principles end up justifying unilateral military interventions by single states. So these states need to convince other states of the justice of their cause, and the best place to do that is the Security Council. But sometimes — and the genocide in Rwanda is one such case — intervention is imperative, yet one or other Security Council power prevents it from happening. In such instances, coalitions of countries may have to persuade each other to act, and they should do so provided that their intervention meets the tests I've outlined. Finally, human-rights principles can never justify a permanent military occupation of another people's territory. If we intervene, we have to get out once the job is done, once victims have been returned to their homes, once the killing has stopped.[20]

I leave it to you to judge whether recent interventions have actually met these tests.[21] Instead, I want to make the more general point that the concept of human rights is a self-limiting kind of authority. Yes, it mandates the use of force in exceptional circumstances. But those who invoke it to justify force are committing themselves to use force with maximum restraint, to seek the consent of victims and the consent of other states, and to leave when the job is done.

Having said all this, I must not pretend that justifications of force will ever be anything but controversial. What some will see as a mission of humanitarian rescue, others are bound to see as an imperialist violation of the sovereignty of a people. People who talk about human-rights principles as if they were the common sense of humankind fail to understand that all rights claims, including those that seem perfectly self-evident to us, are bound to be controversial to others. A belief in human rights is not a faith like a religion, and the authority it confers is not the authority of faith, only the authority of argument. Human rights are not the trump cards that end arguments. In the real business of moral life, there are no trumps. There are only reasons, and some are more convincing than others. If this is true, then the legitimacy of human-rights interventions — the large ones that marshal armies and the small ones that intercede in personal lives — can only ever be limited and conditional. This is a blessing in disguise, for it means that they will never command the kind of consensus that sometimes justifies unlimited brutality.

It would be a mistake, in other words, to think of human rights as a pure and abstract morality. Rights are used to justify acts of power and resistance, and like all such languages, rights talk is open to abuse. Rights talk can be used to justify evil as well as good. But properly understood, it is self-limiting. To say you have a right to do X is to imply the right of Y to resist. To say you have a right, moreover, is to engage in justification, and all justification implies the possibility of rebuttal.

Let me sum up. The first presumption I have argued against in these lectures is that the language of rights is an apologia for force. I am committed to the language of rights for precisely the opposite reason: because it mandates limits to the use of force.

The second presumption I have opposed is the claim that rights language fragments community. I shall have more to say about this in later lectures, because the charge simply won't go away, but for the moment I want to emphasize that rights create reciprocities, and that these reciprocities are the very bedrock of community. Moreover, rights express not only individual claims, but also collective values: above all, the idea that rights are indivisible. If they come for you, they also come for me. That means we must stick together.

The third claim I have criticized in these lectures is that rights are hostile to difference. Marx was simply wrong when he claimed, in 1843, that rights talk reduces us all to abstract, equal individuals, held together by our biological sameness. The claim I would make is the reverse. If the supreme value that rights seek to protect is human agency, then the chief expression of human agency is difference, the ceaseless elaboration of disguises, affirmations, identities, and claims, at once individually and collectively. To believe in rights is to believe in defending difference.

The final argument, most basic of all, is that rights are not abstractions. They are the very heart of our community and the very core of our values. We have them because those who went before us fought for them, and in some cases died for them. Our commitment to rights is a commitment to our ancestors. We owe it to them to maintain the vitality of the right to dissent, the right to belong, and the right to be different. In my next lecture, I want to explain, in more detail, how a single community like ours struggles to reconcile these values. For they make us who we are.

III

THE POOL TABLE OR THE PATCHWORK QUILT: INDIVIDUAL AND GROUP RIGHTS

THE IDEA OF RIGHTS implies that my rights are equal to yours. If rights aren't equal, they wouldn't be rights, just a set of privileges for separate groups of individuals. The essential purpose of any political community based on rights is to protect that equality on behalf of everyone. What holds a nation together, then, is this commitment we each make to treat all individuals the same.

Now the trouble with equality is that no one actually wants to be treated just like everybody else. We want this as a baseline, but we also want more. Each of us wants to be treated equally and to be recognized as different. We want other people to acknowledge us as individuals and as members of groups, to recognize the status that goes with being somebody special. In private life, we usually get this recognition. But we also want our distinctiveness recognized in public. As citizens, we want public officials to pay attention to us as individuals with particular needs. Reconciling the demand that we be recognized as individuals and simultaneously treated as equals is not easy, as doctors, welfare officers, and policemen and -women know to their cost. These people are supposed to be fair without being partial, giving everyone their due without doing anyone any favours. An official who does favours on a regular basis is corrupt. Corruption violates the principle that in this society everyone has rights, but no one ought to have privileges. Again, I'm talking about what's supposed to happen, not what actually does. Everyone, but everyone, is trying to get privileges out of our system. The fact that the system works with any degree of equity and honesty is testimony to the power of equality as an ideal.

This idea of equality, and the notions of fairness that go with it, gives us a particular vision of national belonging. The belonging consists in knowing that everyone shares more or less the same entitlements and the same responsibilities. When we map this ideal of equality onto the countries we actually live in, we get a picture of a nation as a single, homogeneous, and unified political space made up of equal individual units. No region has more power than any other — nor does any group.

It's no accident that this ideal looks like a model from the physics classroom. In late-seventeenth-century England, when political philosophers such as Thomas Hobbes and John Locke were imagining states as communities of equal individuals founded by an original compact in the state of nature, Isaac Newton was imagining physical space in an analogous way: atoms and molecules, units of pure mass, colliding in an undifferentiated medium called space according to the uniform laws of gravity. From that point on, political theory has recurrently sought to model politics as if it were a Newtonian science.

If we move this Newtonian model from the physics classroom to the neighbourhood pool hall, the resulting metaphor looks like this: The pool table is the state. The individuals who make up the nation are the billiard balls. The laws are the bumpers, and the shared territory is the green baize. Now, this model holds that if the individuals in the game are not equal, not able to spin across political space with equal ease, then we should make them so. For the game to work fairly, every individual must be as round and smooth as every other.

And that, of course, is where the trouble starts, and where the analogy between billiards and politics falls down. No one wants to have their edges rounded off, even if that means they can play the game better. They want to play the game on their own terms.

If this is the case, the political problem that every nation has to face looks like this: How can we create a society where everyone has rights without flattening out the differences that give us our identity as individuals and as peoples? How do we recognize group differences without jeopardizing the unity of our country?

Reconciling these objectives is difficult because creating equality and recognizing difference both imply a distinctive kind of political space. The equality project fits well with the Newtonian image of political space as unified green baize. The difference project implies a political space that looks more like a patchwork quilt.

The dilemma we have is that we can't actually choose one to the exclusion of the other. Nations have the characteristics of both. It is basic to the idea of the nation-state that all citizens should have the same rights, and that these rights should apply across the board. There may be different levels of government, but the constitution works out a division of powers so that there is as little overlap and conflict as possible. That's the Newtonian model. No country, however, is only a Newtonian space. Nations are also historical creations, layered with the sediments of time, with old political systems still present just beneath the surface of functioning ones. In Canada, just beneath the political layout created by our act of union in 1867, there are the remains of the four colonial governments that existed before Confederation. Each of these colonies agreed to come into Confederation only if their differences were respected. The one with the greatest number of differences, of course, was the French-speaking colony whose laws, religion, and language were protected by British imperial acts going back to 1774. The Québécois would enter Confederation only if these distinct rights were incorporated into the constitution alongside guarantees to civic equality. This recognition was given, and from the beginning, therefore, Canada was both patchwork quilt and green baize.[1]

The second peoples with original rights of their own were the aboriginals. An imperial proclamation of 1763 recognized their treaty rights, and hence their identity as separate nations, so bringing these peoples into a political confederation should have meant giving them equality as citizens while protecting their communal rights to be different. But that is not what happened. Aboriginal peoples were not given a place at the table when the new political order was created in 1867. Their pre-existing treaty relationships with settler peoples were ignored and their status as nations was dismissed. They were accorded neither the right to be different nor the right to participate in the new union as equals. Having been excluded from the founding of the country, they were made wards of the federal state under the terms of the Indian Act. This act excused them from certain obligations of citizenship, such as paying taxes, while denying them the right to represent themselves, to organize as a free people, and to control the lands and resources they depended on for their livelihood.

In retrospect, it is clear why this happened. As long as aboriginal nations had the power to make war on settler peoples, settlers had a strong incentive to seek peace through treaties. As soon as these settler communities expanded to sufficient size to compete effectively with aboriginal tribes, the settlers claimed exclusive titles to land, ignored treaty agreements, and pushed Native peoples into the hinterlands. Rights were conceded when power was equal; rights were taken away when power flowed to the settler side. Originally, when the two communities met on nearly equal terms, respect flowed from mutual dependence. Respect disappeared when one side ceased to need the other, and when one side was in a position to impose its rule. When power relations changed, so did images of the aboriginal. At first contact, the dignity of Native peoples was as apparent as their power. By the time settlers had established dominion, however, the aboriginal was a dependant. Racial ideology legitimized what sheer force had achieved. Expropriation and the denial of rights were then defended on the grounds that aboriginals were inferior.

Having dispossessed aboriginal nations, settler nations then set out to civilize them. Assimilation was to be the solution for aboriginal inferiority. To that end, aboriginal children were separated from their families, shipped away to residential schools, dressed in uniforms, housed in dormitories, and taught the Christian religion and obedience to Canadian law. The whole process of forced assimilation was much more than pure racism in action. It served a particular idea of democracy. Aboriginal peoples could become Canadian citizens only when they ceased to be aboriginals.

This policy had catastrophic results, and these results are plain to see not just in Canada, but also in Australia, New Zealand, the United States, and Brazil — wherever aboriginal peoples were denied the right to rule themselves. This is more than a story of the damage done by racist contempt and imperialist arrogance. It is also a terrible demonstration of why rights matter. For any people, aboriginal or not, the right to be the member of a nation, to be respected as such, is a vital condition for personal respect, honour, and dignity. When such group rights to nationhood are stripped from a people, the individuals within the group often disintegrate. The lesson that follows is true for aboriginals and non-aboriginals alike: you can't act effectively in the world and take responsibility for yourself unless you respect yourself. And you can't do that unless your identity as member of a people is honoured by the political system in which you live.

The larger lesson is that no matter how they are tried, forced assimilation policies are always a mistake. They either awaken national resistance or succeed at the cost of destroying the morale of the people they tried to assimilate. The message should be clear: you cannot create citizens by force — you must have their consent. The Russian empire sought to Russify the Poles in the nineteenth century. The empire failed. Poland is now an independent nation. The French Third Republic sought to turn Breton peasants into Frenchmen.[2] They failed. The Breton language survives. All peoples will refuse to surrender what is precious to them — land, religion, and language — even when the compensation offered them is equality of citizenship as individuals.

Thanks to the extraordinary historical tenacity with which aboriginal peoples have defended the memory of their nationhood and their treaty rights, the meaning they draw from the failure to assimilate them is clear: they must reacquire their rights of self-government and take responsibility, at the individual and the collective level, for their destiny.[3]

This fundamental lesson, however, is still not accepted by the majority community in Canada. You could blame this on simple racism, but that would be to ignore the real problem. Assimilationist policies would never have been pursued, despite clear evidence of their lack of success, had settlers not believed that a political community must be composed of people who share the same values, culture, and assumptions, and that political equality can be accorded only to those who are recognizably the same. Shedding this belief is hard, for it is an ideal and not just a prejudice.

Aboriginal peoples are not the only ones to have run up against this idea that a political community requires equality and equality has to mean sameness. In the nineteenth and early twentieth centuries, the Québécois were also subjected — it is the only word — to this punitive form of equality as assimilation. Of course, the aboriginal experience was much worse, and it was different in kind. The Québécois were never denied civic equality with other Canadians, but they did experience the humiliation of being a majority within their own province dominated socially and economically by a linguistic minority. Still, the same premise — that to be treated equally, all citizens must be the same — made it impossible to create a country in which French-speakers felt genuinely at home. Recurrently, English-speaking provinces abridged or ignored the rights of French-speakers to educate their children in their own language. Recurrently, Quebecers concluded that a civic union based on equality of rights was a fraud, because it did not allow them to protect what was essential to their survival as a people.

It would be convenient to believe that these problems now belong to an unhappy past. Unfortunately, Canada's political history since 1968 can be told as the story of the unwillingness of the majority to discard the connection between equality, individual rights, and group assimilation. For this link is still held to be the key to keeping the country together. An essential figure in making this strategy explicit was Prime Minister Pierre Trudeau. He believed that rights equality for all Canadians might offer a way out of the emerging constitutional impasse between Quebec and Canada, and between aboriginal peoples and the majority community.[4]

That's how best to understand the rights revolution he spearheaded between 1968 and 1984. There was a deep symmetry in his approach. Faced with the demand by French Canadians that their language and culture receive special protection, Trudeau replied that what required protection was not the rights of a community but the rights of individuals, and that these rights should not be confined to a particular territory, Quebec, but should apply across the country. In legislation that he introduced in 1969, all Canadians were granted the right to bilingual services in French and English in all federal institutions.

With Native peoples, Trudeau believed that the problem lay in their inequality as individuals, which in turn was the fault of the Indian Act. Under its terms, aboriginal peoples were made wards of the national government. They did not enjoy an equality of rights with other Canadians. Their social subjugation and misery could be corrected only if they were accorded full citizenship rights as individuals.[5]

To both groups, therefore, the government offered a

renewal of the national union based on equality of rights. In the aboriginal case, the policy was intended to bring an end to the distinct-group status imposed by paternalist legislation. If aboriginal peoples wished to maintain their customs and traditions, that was a private matter for them to decide. What the government would facilitate was their incorporation as individuals into the national community. In other words, the politics of assimilation remained intact.

In the Québécois case, the intent of bilingual language rights was to break down the barriers between English- and French-speaking Canadians, to assimilate them both into a bilingual national community. Individuals could maintain their group identities as a private matter, but their shared identity would be as citizens of one nation.

In both cases, the Trudeau approach conceived of groups as aggregations of individuals and thought of group identity as a chosen affiliation that could be — and should be — broken off if group purposes conflicted with individual ones.

When Trudeau spoke of a just society, what he meant was a unified national space in which all Canadians would recognize each other as rights-bearers. This is one of the oldest visions of political community. It descends from the Renaissance republics of the Italian city states, and from the heritage of the French Revolution. In this model, national unity is enforced by equal rights and civic assimilation. It is an ideal that defines group differences and group demands as sources of division and that seeks to weaken the hold of groups on individuals in order to incorporate them more fully into the Newtonian space of a national state.

Accordingly, Trudeau sought to patriate Canada's constitution — which was a British act of Parliament — and to entrench within it a Charter of Rights and Freedoms. The charter that he intended to leave as his legacy did not grant group rights to Quebecers or aboriginal peoples. Its entire spirit was to protect individuals from the tyranny of the state and the tyranny of majorities.

For the majority community of English-speaking Canadians, his vision has proven enduringly attractive. No privileges for any groups, but equal rights for all. No distinct societies or peoples, but one nation for all. All provinces to be treated the same. All individuals to be treated with justice. This vision was supposed to pull the country together. In reality, it came close to pulling the nation apart. Why this should be so is of enduring importance, not just to Canada but to all multinational, multi-ethnic states seeking constitutional renewal to reconcile group differences.

The core difficulty is not with the project of civic equality itself. There is no possibility of maintaining a national community of any kind unless every individual within it, regardless of race, creed, sexual orientation, or national origin, can count on an equality of rights. Québécois and aboriginal peoples have no possibility of genuinely belonging to Canada unless they are treated with fairness and respect.

The problem with equality of individual rights is that it is simply not enough. It fails to recognize and protect the rights of constituent nations and peoples to maintain their distinctive identities.

The importance of this is still not apparent to a majority of Canadians. In the eyes of most, aboriginal peoples and French-speakers are minorities. The Canadian Charter of Rights and Freedoms protects the rights of minorities from encroachment. So why, most Canadians ask, are Québécois and aboriginal peoples unwilling to make do with minority-rights protections? The answer is that these groups do not see themselves as minorities at all. Minority-rights protections fail to recognize that these groups are nations, not collections of individuals with similar characteristics.

Most Canadians in the majority community, when faced with this demand for recognition, have little difficulty acknowledging the fact that Native peoples are different and that Quebecers speak a different language. These differences can be welcomed as part of the multi-ethnic, multicultural heritage of Canadians. But recognizing cultural differences is not the point. The recognition these groups seek is political. The claim they make is that unless they enjoy collective rights of self-government over language and land, they cannot securely enjoy their rights as individuals.

Aboriginal peoples and Québécois distinguish the type of claim they are making from the types of claims that immigrants make to defend their own languages and cultures. Immigrants, so their argument goes, arrive in a country as families or individuals, and they accept, as a condition of immigration, that they should learn the language of the majority and obey the laws of the state. Under the provisions of most liberal states, immigrants are entitled to speak their own language at home, to teach their children their native tongue as a second language, to celebrate their festivals, to organize together as community groups, and to practise their religion. But these are not group rights; these are individual rights, based in entitlements to freedom of religion and assembly, and used by groups to maintain a cultural heritage of an essentially private kind. The group rights claimed by aboriginal peoples and Québécois are political, rather than cultural, and they are collective, rather than individual. They are claims to nationhood based on historical priority, on the fact that they were present at the creation of the state, and that the state's very legitimacy depended — or ought to have depended — on their collective consent. Where this consent was never secured — as in the case of aboriginal peoples — it must be secured now.

But this political claim — to self-government in areas essential to a group's survival — poses enormous problems for the majority of Canadians. What's wrong with the Charter of Rights and Freedoms? Canadians want to know. Don't you trust it to protect your rights? Don't you trust us? The demand for special rights appears to cast doubt on the very jurisdiction of these institutions, for neither aboriginal communities nor Quebecers necessarily accept the application of the Charter in matters directly relating to their survival as a people. They say, "What right do you have to impose your rights on us?"

Most people in this country are deeply attached to the

green-baize version of political space: one space for all; one set of rights for all. The minority nations see political space on the patchwork model: self-governing spaces for each; each nation master in its own turf. To this, the majority then asks, "What space remains in common if each nation insists on its own?"

The majority also believes that giving some citizens special rights to protect their language or their lands grants privileges withheld from other citizens. These privileges become a grievance when their exercise excludes other Canadians. If aboriginal peoples gain exclusive rights to land, for example, this may deny other Canadians access to the land or resources in question. Canadian fishermen on both coasts resent the fact that certain waters are claimed as aboriginal fishing grounds under formal treaties signed centuries ago.[6] Here two economically vulnerable groups of citizens are competing for an increasingly scarce resource on which both depend for their livelihood, but one group appears to have a privilege that tilts the balance in their favour. Likewise, in cases where Native nations have established jurisdiction over lands and proceed to levy property taxes on non-aboriginal landholders (who do not have voting rights on tribal councils), these landholders believe that a basic democratic principle — no taxation without representation — is being breached.[7] Such people also believe it is unfair that they are subject to federal, provincial, and aboriginal taxes while their aboriginal neighbours are, in some cases, exempt from all but aboriginal taxation. Many of these disputes are now before the courts.

In a similar vein, Quebec legislation restricts both the use of English in public signage and the free choice of immigrants to choose the language of instruction for their children. To some anglophone Quebecers, these are privileges of a majority that encroach upon the rights of a minority. Since the passage of Quebec's Charte de la langue française, Bill 101, in 1977, there has been recurring conflict between two incompatible visions of how a political community should run, one putting primacy on individual rights, the other on collective rights.[8]

Quebec's language policies appear to violate the ideal of the state's neutrality. Some English-speaking Canadians have had difficulty acknowledging the very idea that any government should privilege the identity of one group, one language, and one culture over any another in its policies. Certainly, Pierre Trudeau saw the Canadian state as a neutral arbiter, and he sought through bilingual legislation to ensure that it favoured neither national community.

In fact, despite its supposed neutrality, the state has always privileged the culture of the English-speaking majority. The very need for bilingual legislation, for example, reveals that the Canadian state had at one time actually favoured English over French in the delivery of services.

No liberal state, therefore, is actually as neutral in its relationship to groups as it purports to be. In supposedly secular and neutral liberal democracies, the designation of Sunday as a day of rest, together with the nomination of Christmas and Easter as public holidays, privileges

Christian denominations over others. Its holidays and public symbols usually reflect the values and culture of the majority.[9]

In responding to these criticisms, there are two ways for a liberal state to go: to reassert neutrality by ceasing to observe rituals and holidays specific to the dominant group, or to recast neutrality as the encouragement of all groups (that is, to become multicultural). Most modern liberal states have taken the second option. In the multicultural response, the state subsidizes the cultural activities of a wide number of groups and designates days of the public calendar to the celebration of the heritage of as many groups as it can. Multiculturalism is intended not to subvert neutrality, but to reassert it in a way that entrenches minority rights to culture against the risks of majoritarian tyranny. But this multiculturalist policy does not amount to an endorsement of group rights. It simply seeks to protect and enhance the capacity of as many individuals as possible to secure public recognition of their different cultures.[10]

The Quebec government, on the other hand, does not purport to be neutral. It argues that its policy of favouring French is not an exercise of majority tyranny, because this particular majority happens to be a minority within the Canadian state, and an even more embattled linguistic minority within the North American continent. Accordingly, the usual strictures against majority domination do not apply. This particular majority is entitled to use state power to favour its own group, the argument goes, provided of course that it does not actively deny the rights of English-speakers.[11]

In assessing the Quebec case for privileging French, there are two tests of the legitimacy of group rights. First, are they absolutely essential to the survival of the group as such? And second, are these privileges accorded in such a way that they do not violate the rights of individuals, either inside or outside the group? It may be hard for English Canadians to admit this, but Quebec's language legislation passes both tests. First, given the fact that minority languages are like rare birds — easily rendered extinct — it's hard to deny the contention that the collective protection of a language employed by 7 million people is essential in a continent of 300 million mostly English-speakers. Such collective protection is important for Quebecers, obviously, but it's important for English-speakers as well, since we also benefit from a country in which linguistic diversity is cherished. Second, the francophone majority *has* respected the rights of minorities in Quebec. Native English-speakers can educate their children in their language at public expense; they can also receive services in their own language. It is true that non-English-speaking immigrant minorities must learn the language of the majority, but this is a standard requirement for immigrants everywhere, and they are not prohibited from using their native language in public or from seeking English-language education at the post-secondary level once they have mastered French.

Group rights have to respect not only the individual rights of other groups — and Quebec language legislation does — but also the individual's rights within the group.

Securing this balance requires political compromise.
French-speaking Quebecers do not have the right to send
their children to publicly funded English-language
schools. If they wish to do so, they must pay for the education themselves. Without this abridgement of the rights
of francophones, and the right of immigrants who wish to
educate their children in English, the very capacity of the
majority to reproduce the French language would be
jeopardized. Yet the sacrifice of individual rights must
secure democratic ratification. And in this case it does.
French- and English-speakers accept, with more or less
good grace, the constraint on the expansion of English-
language education. The balance between group and
individual rights has secured a measure of political
and social peace in Quebec, and to the degree that the
minority values peace, it accepts the compromise.

Elsewhere such compromises are more difficult to
reach. Not all groups accept an obligation to respect the
rights of the individuals within them. Some religious
groups — ultra-Orthodox Jews, fundamentalist Muslims,
and evangelical Christians, for example — have restricted
the rights of women to participate fully in the rituals and
decision-making processes of their faiths. These groups
contend that they exist not to protect the rights of individuals but to obey the rule of God, and since God has
authorized certain forms of female submission, asking
these groups to respect women's rights is to ask them to
sacrifice their very identity for the sake of secular liberal
principles.[12]

Difficult as it is for a secular liberal like me to admit it, these religious communities have a point. So how are we to proceed? Because the state protects these groups — by providing police, social, and welfare services — it has the right to insist that the group respect the basic laws of the state. Yet the state has no right to intervene, except when the rituals involve direct physical harm to individuals. If religions ban women from parts of the ritual, it is no business of the state to enforce their participation.[13] If, on the other hand, members of religious groups seek the state's help to leave or to exercise rights in the society outside, such as seeking an education or marrying someone of their own choosing, then the state has a duty to intervene, simply to enable those individuals to exercise the same rights as other citizens. Likewise, if individuals seek entry to a group and are barred on discriminatory grounds, they should have rights of recourse. In other words, the state should intervene to protect rights of exit and rights of entry, but not to change the character of the group. This non-interventionism is rooted in the idea that the state should be neutral when dealing with lawful ways of living.

The rights that religious groups seek are meant to preserve their cultural autonomy, while the rights sought by national groups, such as the Québécois and aboriginal peoples, are demands for political self-government. These appear to be privileges — that is, rights not granted to other groups of Canadians. How are we to think about rights as privileges?

Privileges are possible, within a rights system, when they are temporary, when they are designed to correct past injustices. The affirmative-action programs accorded women and disadvantaged minorities are privileges in the strict sense that not all citizens have access to them. Yet these exceptions are justified, since their purpose is not to frustrate equality but to make equality a reality for all. By analogy, a majority of Canadians can accept according rights as special privileges to aboriginal Canadians and Québécois as a temporary measure to overcome past disadvantages and correct past wrongs. Quebec language legislation could be justified on the grounds that the French language needed to make up ground and establish a secure future. But once the injustice has been corrected, should the privilege become permanent? The answer depends on the state of the French language in this case. If its survival appears beyond risk or doubt, some revision of the balance between group and individual rights should be called for. Already the legislation has been changed several times to adjust these competing claims. But whether the restriction of English is justified permanently remains a matter of contention among some English-Canadian Quebecers.

There is more support among a majority of Canadians for compensatory affirmative action for aboriginal peoples. The injustices that were done to them are now common knowledge. The need to redress them is perfectly clear. The majority acknowledges it did wrong. It accepts that the minority has an entitlement to redress.

But here, too, a balance has to be struck between the claim of the wronged group and the capacity of the group at fault to pay the claim. In capitalist societies, past wrongs are compensated in two currencies: the language of apology and hard cash.[14] It is well known that neither currency is adequate. When a person has been scarred for life by sexual or racial abuse in an aboriginal school, what apology, what cash settlement, can repair the harm? The natural response is to say that if no currency of account will ever be adequate, the best we can do is make the compensation as generous as possible. Yet generous responses create problems of their own. All of the churches of Canada were responsible for running the aboriginal schools that enforced the federal policy of mandatory assimilation. In many of these schools, brutality and sexual assault were commonplace. Even where they were not, the policy itself was an assault on aboriginal identity, and the results were traumatic.

The churches now acknowledge that both the policy and its execution were indecent violations of the rights of aboriginal peoples. The apologies have been made. The question now is: What compensation should be paid to bring this matter to a close? Individual aboriginal victims have launched suits against the churches, and thanks to the ingenuity of Canada's tort lawyers, the claims for compensation, if granted, would bankrupt most of the organizations in question.[15] The issue then becomes one of whether aboriginal rights to compensation for past injustices should be exercised in such a way as to drive organizations ministering to the spiritual needs of Canadians, Native peoples included, out of business. Now, there are some organizations — fascist political parties, for example — that have been rightly outlawed because they encouraged hatred, contempt, and violence towards other human beings. But the churches simply do not fall into this category — they did not preach racial hatred or contempt. Mistaken as their policies were, their missionary goals did construe aboriginal peoples as fellow human beings. On these grounds, it is hard to see that they deserve to die as institutions.

A balance will have to be found between the rights of aboriginal peoples and the rights of religious communities. Tort proceedings in court are the worst way to reconcile these rights, for the proceedings involve hundreds, if not thousands, of individual suits, and the courts are in no position to balance the collective claims of the two groups involved. The best way to proceed would be to negotiate a three-cornered settlement between Native peoples, church groups, and the federal government. Since group rights are in conflict, they must be reconciled at the political level. The harm that was done to aboriginals was a public wrong, done by our country, through the initiative of the federal government, and if we as citizens want to live in a country that respects itself, then the only way to clear the stain is for us all, and not just the churches, to pay up.

But aboriginal peoples and Québécois are not simply demanding temporary privileges to redress past wrongs. They are demanding permanent rights of self-government that are not enjoyed by other Canadians. The majority concedes the necessity of redress. It does not concede the necessity for permanent self-rule.

These twin demands for self-determination have

divided Canadian society for most of my adult life, and
the conflict reached a crisis between 1982 and 1991.[16] In
1982, the Charter of Rights and Freedoms was created
to bind the country together. English Canadians rallied to
this dry legal document with a degree of fervour that sur-
prised many of its authors. Quebecers did not. They
believed the rights guaranteed them in the Charter were
either unnecessary (since Quebec has its own charter of
rights) or illegitimate (since the province did not agree to
the constitution). Quebecers of nationalist persuasion
remained convinced that the Charter was intended to
abridge their rights as a group. In an attempt to secure the
consent of Quebec to the 1982 constitution, the federal
and provincial governments agreed at Meech Lake to a
deal that would have recognized the distinctiveness
of Quebec society and guaranteed its rights to self-
government in language and other areas essential to its
cultural survival. The deal was turned down by English-
Canadian voters and legislatures because it appeared to
give privileges to Quebec not granted to other provinces,
and because the deal appeared to neglect the demands of
aboriginal groups. In 1992 at Charlottetown, a constitutional deal that sought to protect the group rights of both
aboriginal peoples and Quebecers also failed to win
support in a nationwide referendum. A majority of English Canadians believed that the entrenchment of group
rights would balkanize the country, while a majority of
Quebecers believed that the rights enshrined in the deal
did not protect their essential interests.

The issue of whether group rights should prevail over

individual ones, and the larger issue of whether Canada is a single political space or a multiplicity of national spaces, has proved irresolvable. In this situation of total impasse, a 1995 proposal by the Quebec government that the nation be dissolved altogether lost a referendum in the province by fewer than 60,000 votes.[17] Since that "near-death experience," the only consensus to emerge is that we should postpone everything — whether it be separation or a renewed union — until we have all thought further. The fervent desire to find either common ground or the terms of divorce has been replaced by a tacit contract of mutual indifference.

The whole story may be taken as a parable about the futility of rights talk itself. The minute groups start claiming rights, self-righteousness begins and conflicts become irreconcilable. Nations can't survive too much self-righteousness. Indeed, if a nation were only a community of rights-bearers, it wouldn't survive at all. Happily, nations are more than a tissue of rights. They are highly complex divisions of labour, and as Adam Smith taught us, people collaborate with each other without intending to benefit the country, indeed without intending any other benefit than their own interest. If we think of Canada not just as a rights community, but as a division of labour, a highly efficient economic machine held together by millions of financial, social, and technological connections, we feel better immediately. We may not agree with each other, but we do know how to work together. So our arduous constitutional experience has taught us that countries can endure and cohere, even

on the edge of a rights precipice. That should teach us
that what holds us together is deeper than rights and constitutions and political deals in backrooms. We are
held together by what we do every day. We're also held
together by memory, and by the attachments to land and
neighbourhood, people and places that are dear to us.
These ties are deep, and so there is no reason to despair.
We simply agree to disagree.

Yet we do need to find a better way to resolve our
rights conflicts. We need to find a way to reconcile the
green-baize vision of our country — as a community of
rights-bearing equals — with the patchwork-quilt vision
of our land as a network of overlapping forms of self-
government.

Though these are competing visions, they are not
impossible to reconcile in practice. Group rights that do
respect individual rights of exit and the rights of minorities within the group never pose a problem. Quebec
language legislation is actually a model of a conscientious
attempt by two language communities to work out a reasonable *modus vivendi*. Of course, the larger issue of
Quebec's future within the Canadian federation remains
unresolved, and I will discuss this in my final lecture, but
for the moment I simply want to make the point that
where conflicting visions of group and individual rights
once dogged the Quebec–Canada relationship, a working
resolution of these claims has now been achieved, at
least in respect of language.

Likewise, the agonizing history of group rights claims
by aboriginal peoples has entered a new phase of genuine

mutual recognition and negotiation. Aboriginal groups have consistently argued that their treaty claims to land and resources are based on an ideal of sharing use rights with others, rather than a European model of exclusive ownership. When sharing is the intention, resolution is possible. The problem is how to create the good faith to share between peoples who have such a long history of hurt and injury between them, and in particular, how to adjudicate disputes when sharing fails.

As aboriginal leaders have been saying, and as a recent Canadian Royal Commission on Aboriginal Peoples has argued, the best way to address both issues is through a treaty-making process.[18] This process recognizes the existing treaty obligations of both parties, and it also acknowledges that both parties come to the table as equal nations. The purpose of negotiations is not just to define title to land and resources, and not just to turn over powers of local administration to legitimate aboriginal authorities, but also to find a way to share the sovereignty of the national territory. This issue presents both sides with exceedingly difficult problems of principle. For a Canadian government even to enter into negotiations with aboriginal nations about sharing sovereignty is to concede that the sovereignty they are discussing is a patchwork quilt of overlapping jurisdictions (of which the national or federal power is only one of three). For aboriginals, discussions about sharing sovereignty require accepting the legitimacy of a government that presided over their despoliation as a people. This double process of recognition has been exceedingly hard, and it is not yet concluded. It may take generations before it is completed and a genuine spirit of sharing becomes possible. The treaty process is designed, therefore, as a course of joint problem solving and mutual recognition.

The problem of sharing sovereignty is not just a matter of working out a division of powers — reserving for the federal government such domains as foreign and defence policy, banking, currency, and citizenship, for example, while leaving to aboriginal peoples the administration of local lands, resources, education, infrastructure, and social services. Instead, the key issue is the unity of Canadian citizenship.[19] The non-aboriginal majority believes that the rights protections of the constitution should prevail, while some aboriginal nations deny the jurisdiction of the Charter over such matters as women's rights to participate in decision making or the rights of non-aboriginals who live on aboriginal land. Other aboriginal groups may wish to deny access to their nation on the grounds that the individual seeking membership lacks the right lineage. Yet any use of ethnic, racial, or blood-related criteria for membership in any Canadian group violates Charter rights to civic equality.

In these contentious cases, the right way to approach a solution is not to ask which sovereignty, Canadian or aboriginal, must prevail, but to ask how Charter protections can be reconciled with aboriginal traditions so that the result is legitimate to both parties. And how should joint institutions be designed to do so? Eventually, such matters end up in court, first in the aboriginal courts and then eventually in Canadian superior courts. At all levels, the process of resolution has to be one of intercultural negotiation between equal partners. Equality is mandated by our rights traditions, and so is respect for difference. So Charter protections must be not only respected but also interpreted with due regard to aboriginal custom. The question that has to be answered in this process is not whose rule prevails, but whether the decision that is reached commands the assent of the parties. Achieving legitimacy in the decision should matter more than sovereignty. If we could reinforce the legitimacy of joint decision making, the effect of sharing sovereignty over these decisions would not be to balkanize the country, but the reverse: to increase the felt legitimacy of the decisions and choices that a country has to make.

Most Canadians believe the laws of Canada, especially criminal laws, should be applied and enforced uniformly across all jurisdictions. But if federal or provincial judges sit with aboriginal partners in courts in areas under aboriginal government, and if each group's legal tradition is given the interpretive respect it is owed by the other, it should be possible to arrive at the result that both want (i.e., equal justice for both aboriginal and non-aboriginal Canadians). The strongest incentive to co-operate lies in the plain fact that at the moment they do not, and until Canadian justice acquires legitimacy in the eyes of aboriginal citizens, we will not live in a country that commands their assent.

The process of working out how to share sovereignty is diabolically complicated, protracted, and expensive. Some aboriginal groups are seeking aboriginal government (i.e., control over their own population, lands, and affairs). Here there are substantial problems of institutional competence and experience, and there have been instances where self-government on reserves has been corrupt, inefficient, or nepotistic.[20] Aboriginal peoples would not want their standards of fiduciary responsibility in government to be any less stringent than those required of Canadian municipalities. Other aboriginal peoples, such as those in Nunavut, the vast, new self-governing territory in the Eastern Arctic, are seeking control of a public government — that is, one that rules both aboriginals and non-aboriginals alike. Here the problem is to balance what is in effect ethnic majority rule with minority-rights protections and guarantees of public participation to minorities. And a third group, mostly those resident in cities, is seeking effective control of local services.

Each of these types of self-government is different, each overlaps with other jurisdictions, and each of these overlaps must be harmonized in a spirit of sharing. The units seeking these rights of self-government are often small, divided within themselves and against each other. In one Canadian province alone, there are fifty-one groups, each claiming the title of nation, in negotiation with the provincial government over land claims.[21] Some of these negotiations have been in formal process for more than a quarter of a century. The costs to both sides, in every sense, have been huge. But there is simply no alternative. Assimilation, forced or otherwise, has been tried and rejected. Recent conflicts between aboriginals and non-aboriginals over rights to land have erupted in violence, and in the case of Oka the violence was contained only by the interposition of the army. It is clear that we cannot go on like this. Either we must share power, land, resources, and sovereignty among the nations of this country, or we will founder in civil strife.

But the sharing has to go both ways. The majority's recognition of aboriginal peoples must be followed by aboriginal recognition of the legitimacy of our equal claim to the land. We will not survive if a resentful majority, harassed by guilt-mongering, is simply forced from one concession to another by threats. What is required is a process that builds a mutual and equal recognition, each side publicly acknowledging the other's right to govern and live in peace. At the moment, might lies with the majority and right with the minority. Mutual recognition must rebalance the relationship, with both power and legitimacy finding a new equilibrium. Then, and only then, will we be able to live together in peace in two countries at once, a community of rights-bearing equals and a community of self-governing nations.

IV

RIGHTS, INTIMACY, AND
FAMILY LIFE

DURING THE PAST FORTY YEARS, the rights revolution has penetrated the most intimate spheres of private life. As rights talk moved from the public sphere to the family dinner table and then into the bedroom, it overturned sex roles, the family division of labour, and sexual identity itself. The rights revolution has become a sexual revolution, and in the process, it has transformed all our most important social relationships: between men and women, between parents and children, and between heterosexuals and homosexuals.

All liberal democracies have gone through the same social transformation. The only distinctive aspect of the Canadian pattern has been the speed with which courts and legislatures have responded to demands for children's rights, easier divorce, abortion rights, the equation of marriage and co-habitation, and the full entrenchment of rights to sexual difference. The fact that these rights were conceded speedily does not mean that they were

conceded without a struggle, however. Nor does it mean
that the struggle is over. Women still do not earn equal
pay for equal work and the burdens of unpaid child care
still fall disproportionately upon them. Homosexuals still
do not enjoy the same rights to marry, to adopt, or to
inherit pensions and other assets from their spouses.[1] Yet
even though the rights revolution in private life remains
unfinished, it is hard to imagine that it will not run its full
course. The reason is simply that the rights revolution
appeals to an idea of equality and against this idea there
is no remaining court of appeal.

The demand for equal rights in intimate life is also a
demand for recognition. I've said a lot about rights and
very little about recognition. It's time to define the term.
Recognition is a very Canadian idea, since it was a Canadian philosopher, Charles Taylor, who first put it into
common parlance among political philosophers.[2] To recognize someone in common speech is to put a name to a
face, to single him or her out from a crowd. To be recognized is to emerge from anonymity, to be seen and
acknowledged for what you are. When you are recognized, you cease to be a nobody and you become a
somebody in someone else's eyes. Groups are fighting for
a similar kind of recognition. They want the majority to
re-cognize them, to see them anew, to acknowledge that
they are equal, not only in law, but also in moral consideration. Equality of rights is the precondition for
recognition, but it is not sufficient to ensure it. When individuals and groups seek recognition, they want their
equality recognized, but they want their differences

acknowledged as well. Beyond legal equality, groups seek acknowledgment of the value of their culture, heritage, and distinctive point of view. Struggles for recognition typically require a group of people to recognize themselves first, to overcome their own shame or lack of self-worth and then project an image of themselves as they wish to be seen by the watching world. Once this process occurs, the struggle turns into a demand that the watching world change its view of the group, engage with its own clichéd or stereotyped views and reach out to its members both as equals and as people whose differences from the mainstream are to be acknowledged and welcomed.

The whole difficulty about recognition turns on the question of whether it means acquiescence, acceptance, or approval.[3] When a majority grants a minority rights, is it required to acquiesce to, accept, or actively approve the practices of this group? Certainly gay groups, for example, are asking not just for toleration, but for approval. And approval seems to follow from the idea of equality. But does equality of rights necessarily require equality of approval? The majority has conceded equality of rights to homosexuals, but this seems not to imply approval, merely reluctant tolerance.

In the era of the rights revolution, demands for equal rights have also become demands for approval. Indeed, it might even be claimed that anything less than full approval denies the excluded individual (or group) recognition of his or her status as an equal. But there is a problem here — and it is colloquially called political correctness. One fundamental critique of the rights revolution is that it engenders a coercive culture of ritualized, insincere approval. When every excluded group is demanding both equal rights and recognition, the majority can feel that it is being compelled to accord moral approval to practices that, at best, it only tolerates. So political correctness becomes a code word for a new form of moral tyranny: the tyranny of the minority over the majority. You can't speak of sexual promiscuity among gay people, lest you appear to be demeaning gays in general. You can't speak against affirmative-action programs that favour women, lest you seem to be denying women full recognition and respect. And so on.

Whether these constraints on public speech are actually a form of tyranny is another matter. Anyone with a memory knows that coarse, offensive, and demeaning remarks about women and gays were commonplace in the male culture of recent times. Creating a culture where groups are freed from the dismal drizzle of these remarks cannot be regarded as a serious constraint on the free speech of those attached to these stereotypes. So on balance, the idea that the rights revolution ends in coercive political correctness seems obviously misconceived. Yet closing down a culture of casual and ill-considered abuse is quite different from moving a culture towards full-hearted approval of same-sex activity and positive discrimination in favour of women. Rights equality changes moral culture because groups demand recognition. As they do so, they force sexual majorities beyond toleration towards acceptance and approval. So long as this process is negotiated, so long as it is not presented as a unilateral demand for surrender, rights equality can be followed successfully by full recognition. But if the majority feels coerced into according approval, rather than just toleration, the result is likely to be a backlash. Once the relationship between rights and moral change is understood as a protracted process of intercultural negotiation between majority and minority, it becomes clear that rights are a necessary precondition for recognition, but not a sufficient one. Even if they secure equal rights, same-sex couples may still have to await their fellow citizens' recognition of them as moral equals. The process will take some time and properly should do. But again, it seems hard to imagine that this respect will not follow eventually.

In this lecture, I am examining the intertwined process by which a rights revolution became a sexual revolution, which in turn became a moral revolution driven by a demand for equal recognition. But even this doesn't begin to describe the magnitude of the change that has overtaken private life since I came to manhood in the 1960s. The rights revolution surfed on top of a much bigger wave, which brought with it improved access to higher education for women, the entry of married women into the workforce, the arrival of the birth control pill, and the development of social security systems that cushioned the impact of family breakup.

The American social theorist Francis Fukuyama has called this converging set of moral, technological, demographic, and legal changes "the great disruption."[4] All advanced societies were affected by it, but as Fukuyama argues, Western societies were more disrupted than any other. In a society like Japan, the great disruption did not sweep away traditional marriages or increase the rate of divorce. This fact helps us to see that rights talk in the West did more than ratify social changes that were already under way. It actually helped trigger the social changes themselves. What raised divorce rates in Western society, but not in Japan, was the Western endorsement of values of individual autonomy, which in turn eroded the fabric of female self-sacrifice upon which the family depended as an institution.

Forty years after these changes, we are still trying to take account of their effects. The ledger has many double entries. There is more sexual freedom and more divorce. There are more varieties of sexual identity and more confusion about what kind of sexual beings we actually are. Abortion rights have increased the freedom of women, while at the same time raising bitter and contentious debate about our right to terminate the life of the unborn.[5] There are more types of families — same-sex, single-mother, single-father — and yet more anxiety about whether family intimacy and stability can endure.

In this lecture, I want to tell the story of this double revolution in rights and sexual conduct and ask whether rights talk is weakening or strengthening our capacity to sustain intimate life. We all need intimacy, children especially, but intimacy requires permanence. Is the rights revolution threatening permanence? Is there too much talk of rights in intimate life and not enough talk of responsibility?

Questions like these are not new. Indeed, they are the hardy perennials of modern self-doubt. By modern, I mean any society based on markets and individual rights. In North America and Western Europe, we have been living in such societies at least since 1700 and ever since then social critics have contended that market life endangers stabilizing institutions such as the family. As the great Harvard economist Joseph Schumpeter argued, capitalism depends upon values such as trust and mutual confidence; without these, no one would feel safe enough to enter into contracts and exchanges.[6] Now, the source of such values is the family. But the "creative destruction" of the capitalist investment process recurrently overturns stable ways of life and work based on existing technologies. These convulsions make it difficult for families to maintain continuities of care. If wage pressure and time pressure deplete the emotional reserves of family life, children are less likely to learn the values on which the larger society depends. Children who do not learn how to trust and how to love turn into selfish and aggressive adults. The result, if family breakdown becomes general, is a brutal and uncaring social order. This chain of reasoning is very familiar. There is no more enduring fear in capitalist life than that the system erodes the very values it needs to maintain order.

Capitalism's chronic instability used to be chiefly blamed for harming family life. But newer critiques emphasize the destabilizing effects of abundance. Abundance changes the moral economy of a society by favouring values of consumption over saving, self-assertion over self-restraint, present-mindedness over future-orientation. Abundance has other moral effects as well. Societies of scarcity are obsessed with distribution and therefore with equality; societies of abundance care less about distribution once poverty ceases to manifest itself as absolute deprivation. Paradoxically, abundant societies that could actually solve the problem of poverty seem to care less about doing so than societies of scarcity that can't. This paradox may help to explain why the rights revolution of the past forty years has made inequalities of gender, race, and sexual orientation visible, while the older inequalities of class and income have dropped out of the registers of indignation. Abundance has awakened us to denials of self while blinding us to poverty. We idly suppose that the poor have disappeared. They haven't. They've merely become invisible.

There is little doubt that the rights revolution of the 1960s is the product of the most sustained period of affluence in the history of the developed world. The old virtues, the old limits, lost their legitimacy. The new virtues — self-cultivation, self-indulgence, self-development — acquired the force of moral imperatives. This is the context that explains why the old moral economy of self-denial began to lose not only its economic rationale but its moral dignity as well.

In societies of abundance, the old argument — that capitalism consumes the basis of its own legitimacy — takes on a new twist in the claim that the rights demanded in an era of abundance erode the family structures on which social stability depends.[7] The rights sought in eras of abundance are in fact demands to throw off the order of restraint and repression that prevailed in eras of scarcity. Can family life survive this revolutionary demand for freedom? Is it possible that rights are destroying the very institution that teaches us moral virtue?

A good place to begin the story of the impact of modern rights on intimate life is with divorce. All modern societies liberalized their marriage laws in the 1960s as part of a wave of social legislation, which also included welfare reform and the decriminalization of consensual same-sex activity between adults. In Canada, the Divorce Act of 1968, the first national divorce law in our history, permitted termination of marriage on grounds of adultery and cruelty or if couples had already lived apart three years. When the act was amended in 1985, this waiting period was reduced to one year.[8] This provision effectively introduced no-fault divorce into Canadian life and the impact was felt immediately. By the 1990s, one marriage in three in Canada was ending in divorce. The results, for children, have been dramatic. It is estimated that half of the children currently growing up in developed nations will see their parents divorce by the time they are eighteen.[9] Most troubling is the possibility that rising divorce rates are correlated with rising levels of child abuse. This would be the case if children turned out to be more at risk of abuse from step-parents than from their natural kin. It is not clear whether child abuse is actually increasing, but if there were a correlation between such an increase and rising divorce rates, then the rights revolution would be having disturbing effects indeed.

As divorce rates have risen, so have rates of cohabitation, couples living together outside of marriage.[10] The rise of cohabitation reveals the new rights that have been asserted in intimate life since the 1960s: the right to found and dissolve intimate partnerships at will and to do so without the intervention of church, state, or family. Cohabitation was a declaration of sovereignty by the couple, an assertion that they, rather than the state, would define the terms of their relationship. In fact, of course, as these relationships foundered, cohabiting couples, like married ones, found themselves returning to the state (i.e., to the courts) to seek the rights to maintenance, child support, and family property provided by formal marriage. Indeed, as the incidence of cohabitation has increased, the pressure has grown to accord cohabiting couples the same rights as married ones. So the course of the rights revolution has had an ironic outcome. Couples might have wanted to keep the state out of their relationships at the point of getting together, but they discovered that they needed to get the state back in as an adjudicator when these relationships fell apart.

Forty years into the rights revolution, we are no longer sure what role courts and legislatures should play in family life. Should the law be promoting a certain standard of family life, or should it just be serving *in loco parentis* for children at risk from family violence and breakdown? This issue has turned many people's politics upside down. Feminists who once insisted that the state had no business in their bedrooms now clamour for state intervention to protect women against family violence.

Conservatives who once denounced the nanny state now plead for government to enforce frayed moral standards. As for liberals, many secretly wonder whether their revolution has gone too far.

The controversy over whether there should be laws against corporal punishment in families brings out all our perplexities about the relationship between state and family life. Some people believe that a state ban on corporal punishment would align the force of the law on the side of a crucial moral principle. Others maintain that punishing parents who use physical correction against children would be an invasion of family life. An Ontario court judge recently ruled against outlawing physical correction of children on the grounds that it infringed on the family's essential margin of autonomy.[11] It seems clear that the right of the child that needs defending is the same one accorded adults: the right to live a life free of fear. Children should respect their parents but never fear them, for fear always casts a shadow of mistrust over love and care. Children will never trust the love of someone who has made them frightened. So we do not want to strike children unless there is simply no other way to stop them from doing harm to themselves or others. But as soon as we concede that some forms of mild and non-harmful physical punishment may occasionally be necessary, it becomes difficult to enforce a distinction between legitimate and illegitimate correction. Do we need to? There are already sufficient laws to protect children against physical abuse, and these allow the state to take children into care. So their rights already have protection. Additional legislation may only multiply the number of wrongful prosecutions of parents, which would weaken rather than strengthen family life.

What this story illustrates best, I think, is that the state has only a limited capacity to protect children. We already have a vast apparatus for child protection — social workers, welfare officers, family physicians, court-appointed guardians, and so on — but despite the (mostly) conscientious efforts of those who work in this area, our society continues to be disgraced and shamed by the unheard screams of children. Sometimes these cries are very close by: through the party wall, across the garden fence, in the next aisle of the supermarket. What this says to me is that rights are not enough. The welfare state is not enough. Indeed, sometimes we enact rights in the statute books and the result only weakens our responsibilities. This might be the case with children in danger of abuse. The child-protection bureaucracy, necessary as it is, sometimes confiscates responsibilities that properly lie in society itself, with neighbours, friends, and good-hearted strangers. Ultimately, child protection is not up to the state; it is up to us. If we see a child being beaten, we must raise the alarm. A rights revolution is meaningless unless it calls forth our civic courage to intervene when we know we should.

Inevitably, the rights revolution — and the sexual revolution that went with it — produced backlash. Since the mid-1970s, conservative politicians and social analysts have been arraigning the liberal reforms of the 1960s and condemning their consequences. The backlash has

reversed the usual conservative position on rights. Conservatives used to be strong exponents of individual
rights, since rights define the limits of state intervention
and conservatives were anxious to set limits on the power
of the post-war state. Liberals, on the other hand, used to
be more hostile to individual rights talk, because some
rights, especially property and privacy rights, were
invoked by conservatives to resist crucial liberal objectives, such as the establishment of graduated income tax
and the creation of a welfare state. The revolution in family life has turned this alignment upside down. Now
conservatives say that rights have gone too far, while
liberals are trying to stay the course of a rights agenda.

The problem with liberal rights talk, conservatives
argue, is that it individualizes people. Once people begin
speaking about their rights, they start counting the costs
of all relationships with other human beings that involve
sacrifice. And family life is based on sacrifice: parents
devoting years to the care of children when they might
prefer to be furthering their own interests, and husbands
and wives devoting themselves to each other when other
persons and possibilities beckon.

This argument has something to say for it, but not
much. Conservatives are wrong to suppose that rights
talk invalidates sacrifice itself. Even we heartless liberals
need intimacy and we know that we cannot have intimacy without sacrifice. These sacrifices, both moral and
material, are worth bearing when they are borne mutu-
ally, when both partners share the load, and when the
result of equal sacrifice is renewed affection. Much of

the complaint about family life focuses not on sacrifice per se, but on inequality of sacrifice. This inequality is not imagined: it is painfully real. In Canada, statistics show that even now, after a generation of feminist progress, 70 percent of the burden of caring for children, the aged, the disabled, and the sick falls on women, most of whom receive no pay for these essential tasks.[12] These enduring facts help us to see that the revolt against family life in the 1960s was a revolt not against sacrifice but against inequality of sacrifice. And to judge from the statistics, the revolution remains unfinished.

But feminism was much more than a revolt against inequalities of sacrifice. It was also a revolt against certain kinds of sacrifice, notably the sacrifice of female identity. Young women coming of age in the 1960s looked back on the lives of their own mothers, women who had come of age in the Depression and the Second World War, and felt that they had thrown away their lives for the sake of their husbands and children. The sacrifice that had been made was of their very selves. This was the cardinal wrong that had to be righted. When daughters raised this issue, the results were often painful. What daughters accusingly called sacrifice, some mothers poignantly felt as fulfilment, at least of a kind. But sometimes the confrontation between generations ended with both feeling the same sense of injustice.

As a man who came of age in the late 1960s, I was deeply affected by feminist rights talk, and by this reckoning between mothers and daughters. Like many men, I was soon to go through my own version of *Fathers and*

Sons. The central idea I absorbed then — chiefly, if not exclusively, from feminism — was that each of us has a right to choose the life we lead and that we must fight to exercise this right against all comers. This could be called the ideal of authenticity.[13] In the name of this ideal, we all went off to find ourselves. This meant getting away from family, career, and society, and going in search of the self's authentic impulses. Sometimes the results were laughable: the 1960s cult of authenticity produced dull conformity in no time. We all went in search of ourselves and ended up in graduate school. Even those who dropped out tended to end up conforming to a non-conformist lifestyle.

For many of us, even those for whom the 1960s were either an episode or just a memory, the ideal of authenticity exerted a powerful influence on our very idea of what it was to have a life and a career. Authenticity taught us that we had a duty to ourselves and not just to others, and that in the face of a conflict between these two duties, we would sometimes have to choose for ourselves — against children, families, lovers, and friends.

So to summarize the argument so far, two moral ideas were the heart of the rights revolution in private life: first, that family sacrifice is unjust unless it is equal; and second, that each of us owes a duty to ourselves, and this is equal to the duty we owe to others. Let's admit immediately that these were highly contentious values. Conservative social critics would argue that these ideals are just fancy ways to justify selfishness. What I have been calling the rights revolution, conservatives would dismiss as the permissive revolution. The cardinal vice of permissiveness is wanting rights without responsibilities: wanting sex without love, wanting intimacy without commitment, and worst of all, wanting children without being willing to care for them. Liberalism, so the argument goes, has made a devil's bargain with permissiveness. In the name of an ethics of authenticity, rights talk is actually undermining the very possibility of moral behaviour, since it appears to authenticate every selfish impulse: to quit marriages when they don't work, to abandon children when work calls, to flee responsibility when pleasure beckons. To make matters worse, conservative critics say, the state colludes in this selfishness by providing welfare benefits for unmarried mothers, so that the costs of irresponsibility are paid not by the guilty, but by the hard-pressed taxpayer.

When divorce is the norm, conservatives argue, children grow up in a moral world in which all trust is conditional, because betrayal is always possible.[14] According to the conservative critique, we risk producing a future generation of children who trust so few people that they no longer start families themselves.

And even when families survived the permissive revolution, conservatives argue, they were damaged by it. The mistake was believing that the family could be run as a community of rights-bearing equals. Children are not the equals of their parents; they need limits and rules. Permissive parenting, on a rights-equality model, so it is argued, has produced a generation of young adults who came of age in the 1990s, never having learned the meaning of self-discipline.

Let us grant what we can to the conservative counter-attack. Let us grant that freedom is not a licence to do whatever you please. Let us insist that fathers and mothers must know how to say the word no; that moral life for children begins with the understanding of limits; that any person who embarks upon the adventure of marriage must judge the result not by happiness alone, but by other, more arduous standards, such as staying the course. None of this is alien to the liberal temperament or inconsistent with a commitment to rights equality between men and women. Indeed, it is impossible to envisage marriage surviving at all unless both partners strive towards equality.

The conservative critique of permissiveness has its points, but it is reactionary in the strict meaning of the term. It wants to turn the clock back, and to do so by means of coercive legislation — such as making divorce more difficult and penalizing single parents — which would violate conservativism's own commitments to the freedom of the individual. A liberal position is simply more consistent with that commitment. Moreover, a liberal rights culture does not obliterate responsibilities: it presumes them. To father a child is to shoulder responsibility for its upbringing. If a father abandons his family and fails to pay maintenance, he should be pursued and, if he still fails to pay up, punished. If pregnant mothers so abuse themselves with drugs and alcohol that they damage their children, they should feel the penalties of the law.[15] A state whose child-protection agencies fail to pin responsibility on defaulting parents, and whose welfare institutions then mutely step in to cope with the consequences, is undermining the link between rights and responsibilities that makes a rights culture consistent with public order. On this issue, a liberal and a conservative will see eye to eye.

But on others, the divide is unbridgeable. What conservatives see as the collapse of the family, liberals view as its mutation into new forms. Nowadays, there are many types of good parents and many types of good families: nuclear, extended, single-parent, same-sex. The fact that there are many types of families does not mean that there are no longer any fixed standards about what a good family is. The test of goodness is loose but evident: it's a community where each member receives and displays lifelong moral concern for the well-being of everyone else. The key is not love necessarily, or hugs, or sentimental Disney eyewash, but an enduring moral commitment. A child needs to feel that her development matters intensely to another person, and that this person will stay the course with her to ensure that she develops as best she can. What a liberal insists upon is the idea that it is possible to reconcile a commitment to absolute standards of care and responsibility in family life with a faith that these standards can be met by a wide variety of persons and a wide variety of possible family forms.

So-called family values, as propagated in the rhetoric of North American popular entertainment, pulpit sermonizing, and political homily, are a downright tyranny. They make people feel inadequate, ashamed, or guilty about their inability to conform to what is in fact a recent, post-war suburban norm of family domesticity.

We need family values all right, but the ones we actually need must be pluralistic. We need to understand that the essential moral needs of any child can be met by family arrangements that run the gamut from arranged marriages right through to same-sex parenting. Nature and natural instinct are poor guides in these matters. If good parenting were a matter of instinct, families wouldn't be the destructive institutions they so often are. It is frequently the case that perfect strangers turn out to be better parents or step-parents than natural ones. This is not always the case, of course, as the incidence of abuse by step-parents attests.

The point is not to invalidate one type of parent. Instead, it is to insist that ideology will not help us here: if we insist that one category or type of parent will always do a better job than any other, we are certain to be wrong. Same-sex parents have taught us that there is no necessary relationship between heterosexuality and good parenting. The question to be asked in every case is not what kind of sexual creatures these parents are, or even what kind of biological or other relationship they have to these children, but what kind of parents they are. The test of goodness here is the capacity for sustained moral concern and to be willing to make reasonable sacrifices for the sake of children's interests. A family is not a bus station: children will not develop well when there is no continuity of care and concern. Continuity implies sacrifice but reasonable sacrifice doesn't necessarily mean putting children's interests first. No model of family life will work if it is based on unequal and unlimited sacrifice. As a moral training ground, families ought to teach the lesson that no one's interests should automatically come first and certainly not the children's.

Getting any of this to work is not easy. None of us is always capable of unconditional moral concern for another human being, but some surprising people routinely do it better than we do. Opening our eyes to the different ways other families work is more useful than despising those who do things differently. Pluralism does not mean relativism. It means humility.

But, conservatives say, even if one admits the viability of same-sex, single-parent, or divorced families, the problem is that these new family forms do not endure. They are eaten from within by the liberal ideology that family life should be satisfying, and that if it isn't, each member should exercise their right of secession.

Let us acknowledge that fathers — and mothers — are deserting their families in the name of "finding themselves," and that children are paying a high price for the inability of adults to reconcile duty and desire, freedom and responsibility. As a father, I find it hard not to be pained by the statistics about modern fatherhood and divorce in Canada: mothers get custody of children in 86 percent of cases, and more than 40 percent of children in Canada's divorced families see their fathers only once a month. Even when both parents remain present in their children's lives, research in England shows that, in families where both spouses work, mothers spend ninety minutes a day with their children and fathers only fifteen minutes. The same pattern must be broadly true among Canadian working families. Here the ideal of authenticity — of both parents seeking lives that fully express their capacities — risks being purchased at our children's expense. But let's stop lamenting these trends as if we were powerless to do anything about them, as if they were some malign kind of fate. We've made the rights revolution, and we need to fix it. And that is precisely what working families are trying to do. There isn't a responsible working couple I know who aren't conscious of this conflict between what they owe themselves and what they owe their children. Many of them have tried to have it all and discovered that they need one item more than any other: time with each other.

Many families do break up under the strain of these competing claims. Some parents simply abscond altogether. The disappearing dad — who neither pays child support nor visits his children — is a fact that cannot be denied, and his absence from his children's lives can have painful effects.[16] These effects do not just harm children, of course. They also harm women. Divorce has become a multiplier of inequality in Canada: deprivation is heavily concentrated among single mothers with children.[17]

Yet this crisis is too complex to be blithely blamed on "deadbeat dads" alone. In hearings before a parliamentary committee in Canada in 1998, groups of fathers bitterly complained that they were bearing the brunt of public blame for what has happened to the family. In fact, they claimed that they were discriminated against. Courts were favouring mothers over fathers in custody disputes, and the divorce process was being abused by lawyers despoiling working men of their assets. These groups demanded that the "custody and access" regime created by the Divorce Act of 1985 be replaced with a "shared parenting" regime in which both parents are given equal rights to bring up their children.[18] These are sensible and overdue suggestions, and the fact that they're being made shows that men and women are struggling to correct the rights revolution, so that equality works for everyone.

In facing up to these issues, liberals also need to face up to their responsibilities. Let us acknowledge that the rights revolution must shoulder some share of the blame for family breakup and its consequences in our society. Even if a lot of other factors also come into play — the pressure of work in capitalist society, the mobility that market success requires of many families — it has to be true that we divorce more frequently than our grand-parents because of the kinds of freedom we take for granted, and hence the kind of persons we have become. We do believe we have a right to happiness; we do believe we want to live our lives instead of silently enduring them; we are much more explicit than our grandparents about wanting sexual happiness and a wide variety of sexual experience.

But the conservative critique, which denigrates these desires as selfishness, gets us nowhere. People can and do repent of selfishness and they can turn their back on appetite. But the rights revolution has been propelled by something stronger than appetites: it's propelled by the values of authenticity that shape our ideas of what a good life should be. The divorce rates tell us that men and women are no longer willing to suffer and be still. Our rights culture endorses complaint and it dignifies discontent. It offers moral legitimacy to departure.

There is a deeper conflict than our parents' generation imagined between being faithful to others and being faithful to ourselves. It is entirely possible to be true to others — your spouse and your children, for example — and betray yourself. By betrayal, I mean giving yourself to others in ways that sacrifice your talents, your special gifts, your unique ability to contribute. If you betray yourself in this way, you then render yourself useless to others, incapable of carrying out your duties and responsibilities with conviction and self-respect. It is this moral insight — more than just sexual temptation or appetite — that drives so many modern marriages onto the rocks. Marriages can survive sexual temptation. They can even survive betrayal. What they cannot survive is either partner believing they have betrayed something essential about themselves. We ought to be candid enough to admit that when a marriage forces a couple to betray themselves, it deserves to fail.

Even if we should accord respect to divorce, let no one suppose that there can ever be such a thing as a painless one. Even those who make a happy escape can be burdened for the rest of their lives by a real sense of sadness and failure. And the harm done to children is real, though this harm must be evaluated against what might be called the contra-factual harm: what would have happened had the parents stayed together. Indeed, all one can ever say about divorce is that it can teach children something sad but true about life: that love is not eternal, that trust can be lost as well as won, that betrayal is a fact of life. Some believe that children should always be sheltered from these facts. But I don't see why innocence should enjoy these moral prerogatives, because I don't see why concealing the truth helps children. And besides, children know more than we think. Anybody who breaks up a marriage certainly learns one thing: if you cannot justify divorce to your children, you cannot justify it to yourself. And justify it you must. But this truth is underpinned by another: that a modern family is a realm of moral equals, each with claims and each with rights, one of which is a right to justification.

We owe children truth; we owe them reasons for our conduct. Sustained moral concern implies helping them to understand us as the imperfect but struggling agents we are. Divorce takes everyone off the pedestal. But why did we put ourselves on the pedestal in the first place? Parents needn't be heroes — moral or otherwise. Nor should they be friends. They should be parents.[19]

Children do have rights. They have the right not just to be sheltered and cared for and protected from abuse, but also to be treated as moral agents in their own right, with intentions, purposes, and visions of the world that we should not presume are identical to our own. A liberal ideal of parenting puts empathy at the heart of modern family life — that is, no longer taking children for granted, no longer assuming that they should be the silent and obedient witnesses to the godlike dramas played out above their heads, but acknowledging that they are incipient adults whose minds must be read, whose hearts must be understood, and whose love must be earned.

Will a society of children raised in divorced families be a society in which individuals no longer know how to trust one another? This will happen only if we lie to them, only if we pretend to be happy when we're not, only if we fail to treat their emotions with the respect they deserve. Only if we fail to give them what we know we need ourselves: the continuous light and warmth of sustained moral concern.

Only a complacent person could possibly be happy with the state of modern married life and the family. The conservative blames the rights agenda for creating discontentments with family life that didn't exist before. But this is false. The unhappiness was there; the rights revolution simply enabled men and women to act on the unhappiness they once felt powerless to change. What rights have done is to enlarge people's sense of themselves as agents: empowering them to think of their urgent needs as entitlements and giving dignity to their complaints about the unfairness and injustice of family life. But this injustice exists. It cannot be conjured away by greater acts of will and self-repression and it cannot be dispersed by the law.

Nor can we go back on what we have already done. The changes in family life are not a transient effect of 1960s fashion; they are not the consequence of some blind

descent into moral selfishness. They are here to stay and
we need to make the promise of moral equality in intimate life real for all of our citizens. Families that divorce
need help so that parenting responsibilities can be
genuinely shared, not reluctantly conceded in rigid
custody-and-access schemes that end up dividing children from their parents. We need to create new cheap and
efficient institutions that mediate family conflict instead
of impoverishing families with exorbitant legal costs.
Instead of abandoning the equality agenda that began in
the 1960s, we need to complete it. Same-sex couples
should be entitled to the same rights of marriage, adop-
tion, and parenthood as other-sex couples and they
should be held to exactly the same standards of responsibility and accountability.

Families that work need help to survive — help
that includes decent public education, publicly funded
daycare, universal health care free at point of need, and
accident and unemployment insurance. Families also
need respite from the devouring impact of work and
stress on intimate life. We need to change the employment laws so that family life is not squeezed between the
millstones of two precarious incomes. The key goal of our
social policy should be to give families the time they need
to be together.

In the new century, most families that survive do so
not by jettisoning the values of their parents, but by rein-
venting them and rebalancing the division of labour.
They balance rights against responsibilities, seek to equal-
ize sacrifice, and manage to impose rational limits on

children's behaviour. But no vision of family values has a chance of commanding genuine assent — and that is the test of an ethic's legitimacy — unless it accords respect for the individual's needs *against* the devouring claims of family life.

Much as deficit-reducing conservatives may lament the fact, the test of serious moral commitment to the family is a willingness to spend public money. Effective child protection, universal access to health care, affordable child care, first-rate primary and secondary education — these are the building blocks of the protective arch that society must raise over its families. This institutional arch doesn't come cheap, but those exponents of family values who won't stump up for it are just engaging in cheap talk.

The rights revolution has not launched us on a slippery slope towards nihilism and social collapse. We are simply trying, with as much success as failure, to live by the twin ideals of equality and authenticity, to fashion lives that reflect our choices and do not depend on thwarting the lives of others. There is wreckage at our feet, but the new forms of family and intimate life that are emerging do what these institutions have always done: sustain us with a shared experience of moral concern. There is much that we could do better, and we had better acknowledge, sooner rather than later, that we cannot have it all. If we want happy children and happy spouses, we had better fight back the claims of work; if we want to be treated equally, we will have to treat others equally; if we want our children to respect us, we will have to respect their need for rules and order. What I think cannot be changed is our sense of ourselves as free agents: the idea that all family members have rights; that we have duties to ourselves, as well as to others; that no one is there to serve, honour, obey, and suffer in silence; that we are committed to perceiving each other not as equals — since parents and children cannot be equals — but as moral entities entitled to reasons, the best ones we can devise. The liberal proposition is that children deserve reasons as much as love, and that reasons are a form of love.

It is often said that we should beware of what we want, because we are likely to get it. We need to see our anguish and disarray about the family as a struggle to face up to the consequences of having got what we wanted. We wanted freedom and we should stop apologizing for it. We must simply pay its price. As Isaiah Berlin once said, freedom is a chilly virtue: it is not justice, equality, or a quiet life; it is merely freedom.[20] Almost everybody is frightened of it. And almost everybody would restrict somebody else's freedom if he could get away with it. Freedom is not the only moral virtue, not the only moral priority, but it happens to be the precondition of all the others. An agent who is not free cannot be a responsible one at all. If we value responsibility, then we need to have the courage to embrace our freedom. It is the very condition of responsibility, not to mention self-respect, and hence the very basis of an authentic life. The rights revolution has been in the service of freedom and we need to have the courage to continue with it until we can genuinely say that everyone shares its benefits and not just its costs.

V

RIGHTS, RECOGNITION, AND NATIONALISM

IN THE COURSE OF THESE LECTURES, I've retold the history of our country since the 1960s as a story of the struggle by different groups of citizens for rights and recognition. In this final lecture, it's time to draw together the argument and ask a basic question: Has the rights revolution brought us closer together as a nation or driven us further apart?

The answer to the question depends on whose point of view you take. In these lectures, I've taken the point of view of the rights-claimants in these struggles: women seeking sexual and economic equality, aboriginal peoples seeking recognition of their title to land, ethnic minorities seeking protection of their culture, and same-sex couples seeking rights equivalent to those afforded heterosexuals. From their perspective, the history of the past forty years is a story of freedom painfully fought for and far from achieved. Unity, by and large, has not been their concern.

From the viewpoint of the bystander majority, however, the rights revolution has often seemed less about emancipation than about fragmentation, with the Canada they once knew taken apart and reassembled into a fractious collection of rival rights communities: gays versus straights, aboriginal peoples versus non-aboriginals, French-speakers versus English-speakers, immigrants versus native-born, abled versus disabled, rich versus poor. The rights revolution empowered these groups at the price of disempowering the majority. When a majority feels it is weakened, it is natural for it to believe that the country has been weakened as well.

Minorities have won recognition, and now it is the turn of the majority to look around and ask, in astonishment, whether it recognizes itself. Where is the majority any more? Who are we? Once we thought we knew: white, heterosexual, family-oriented, native-born people who were Canadians first and anything else second. Now the population is cross-cut with identities — sexual, racial, religious, and ethnic — making it difficult to speak of a Canadian majority at all. This may be one reason for the belief, widely held among our elites, that our country has become ever more difficult to govern. The essential work of national politics is creating majorities (i.e., national coalitions of interest). As the rights revolution fragments the majority, it fragments the coalitions that keep the country together.

The rights revolution also turns politics into an exchange of recrimination between victims and their supposed oppressors. It's not that there aren't real victims out there; the problem is that the majority has genuine difficulty accepting the idea that present generations remain responsible for the harms committed by past ones. How long must the Canadian majority continue to pay for the abuses done to aboriginal peoples in times past? How long must it do penance for racism, sexism, and other forms of injustice? It is clear that for many Canadians, the debate over past injustice produces not mutual recognition but resentment. Victim and oppressor become co-dependent, locked into their roles and unable to shed them. The victim minorities resent depending on the majority for redress. The majority resents depending on the minority for forgiveness. Since forgiveness would foreclose future claims, victims tend to withhold it; since redress implies culpability, it too is withheld. So the politics of argument is replaced by a politics of blackmail and stonewalling. Many in the majority Canadian community who have felt themselves put in the dock by the incessant accusations of various victim communities do not see the rights revolution as a story of a successful fight for inclusion by the excluded. Instead they see it as a story of how a once strong country was fragmented.

Before we determine whether the rights revolution has been destructive of national unity, we should notice that focusing on the rights revolution and its consequences offers a different perspective on the unity issue than the one we became used to before the rights revolution began. The unity debate of the early 1960s was almost entirely about whether Quebec's demands could be met within the framework of the Canadian federation.

No one else's claims belonged in the frame, certainly not those of aboriginal peoples, women, people of colour, and same-sex groups. None of these groups was perceived as offering any kind of political challenge to the unity of the country. The only such challenge came from Quebec, and the holy place where this challenge was addressed was the preserve of the high priests of federalism: constitutional lawyers and federal and provincial bureaucrats who knew by heart every arcane clause of the British North America Act, and could tell you, as the old joke used to have it, whether having sex in Canada was a provincial responsibility or a federal one.

The high priests went about their work for a century and a quarter, interpreting the sacred texts and waving the incense of rhetoric in the direction of the congregation, but they did not succeed in keeping the country together. Indeed in 1995, we came within 60,000 votes, in the Quebec referendum, of beginning the dissolution of our country. By then, the high priests had lost control of the rituals of unity. Quebec's battle with Canada had become fused with all the other battles for recognition. At the constitutional talks on Quebec's future, aboriginal and women's groups won a place at the negotiating table. Quebec discovered that it could not secure its demands unless aboriginal peoples and women also won theirs. As these rights claims converged in one negotiating forum, the result was deadlock. A bilateral discussion between Quebec and Canada has been transformed into a multi-dimensional chess game. This "rights frenzy" — that is, the proliferation and entanglement of rights claims — has made many commentators question our very capacity to keep the country together.[1]

But this negative point could also be put positively. Instead of fragmenting the country, rights talk has actually made the national-unity process more democratic. By forcing their way into the negotiations on national unity between 1987 and 1991, women and aboriginal peoples secured a right of participation not just for themselves but for all Canadians. Future constitutional change will have to be ratified by a national referendum. The citizens have forced their way into the inner sanctum and whatever arcane rituals of accommodation are enacted there in the future will require the citizens' consent.

This particular point about rights demands and democracy could be generalized. Not all of the battles fought by minorities have been only on behalf of their own groups. Sometimes, the rights that have been won have been won for everyone. For example, women were never fighting just for themselves; they were fighting for their children, and even for the men in their lives. Likewise, the Charter of Rights and Freedoms is not just a collection of entrenched rights for various linguistic, sexual, and aboriginal minorities. It standardized rights for all citizens. To the degree that rights struggles for particular groups enhance or clarify the rights of all citizens, they strengthen, rather than weaken, the country.

Even when the rights that are gained are exclusively for the use of a particular group, all may benefit indirectly from the fact that the political process becomes more inclusive, and therefore better able to respond to public needs and aspirations. Thus only the disabled specifically benefit when their rights of access and mobility are granted, but the rest of us benefit in a general way too. We benefit because the disabled are freed from dependency relationships that embarrass them and us. Once their mobility rights are guaranteed, they can look after themselves and establish relationships with the rest of us on a basis of genuine equality. The second benefit to us of specific mobility rights for the disabled is that they help our democracy to work better. We are not required to represent the interests of the disabled, since they can do it themselves. And those who represent themselves invariably do a better job than anybody else.[2]

In other cases, however, the majority is less convinced that it has benefited from the rights revolution. Other battles — such as those for language rights, aboriginal title, and sexual enfranchisement — have seemed not to benefit the majority, but rather to force it to cede power and cultural authority. The cultural authority in question is the right of the majority to define what the country "stands for," and how it is seen by itself and the rest of the world. So on questions of sexual morality, the impact of the rights revolution has been to diminish the power of the heterosexual majority to define what is normal and normative in personal life. On questions of our national history and self-image, the impact of the aboriginal revolution has been to force the Canadian majority to face up to the spectre of racism in our national past. When groups get rights, in other words, they also get the right to change the national story, and when they do so, the results can be painful. Once rights are granted, the majority has to live with the truth, and the truth can hurt.

In more direct and immediate ways (i.e., through tax dollars), the Canadian majority has had to pay for the rights revolution. For many in this bystander majority, it seems that the Canadian state is being treated like a kind of general store, situated at a dusty crossroads where federal and provincial power meet, which every passing traveller feels free to loot in the name of some rights claim or other. Certainly the cost of meeting rights claims — and these claims include rights to welfare, employment insurance, pay equity, and aboriginal title — helped to increase the federal deficit. By 1995, the problem demanded a solution. But the solution — cutbacks to federal services — further weakened the welfare and regional adjustment programs that hold the country together. In this way, meeting rights claims has not always strengthened the sinews of national unity.

The revival of English-Canadian nationalism in the 1980s and 1990s is a reaction to these trends, not just to Quebec nationalism. The mood of English Canada has settled into a single angry demand: enough is enough. This anger is focused not just on Quebec, but also on aboriginal peoples and other rights-claimants. Enough concessions, enough negotiations, enough rights already. There is a new sympathy for symmetrical federalism: equal rights for all provinces and all individuals; no special status for anybody. What I've called the pool-table version of national political space seems to promise an end to the politics of victimhood and blackmail. Strict equality of individual rights would bring us together. We would cease to recognize each other as competing rights communities and instead see ourselves as fellow citizens.

In an earlier lecture, I argued that this symmetrical version of rights doesn't work. It's not true to our history. We simply are a patchwork quilt of distinctive societies. Quebec is entitled to recognition as a distinctive society and its language laws, immigration statutes, and education provisions should be different in order to protect what is different about the province. There also need to be special language laws, as well as French-language education, for New Brunswick because of the size and importance of its Acadian minority. Provinces with large aboriginal populations, like British Columbia, may have to devolve power over land and resources in ways that are different from other provinces. Each situation is different and each needs to be addressed with special provisions.

Yet recognition of distinctiveness does not have to fragment the country. What ought to balance these distinctive provisions is a politics of reciprocity. If Quebec is granted certain rights in respect of its language and culture, the rest of the country has a right to expect the province to protect the cultures, languages, and religions of its minorities. Reciprocity rather than strict symmetry for all is the way to move beyond a politics of concession and threat into a process of mutual recognition, in which each side acknowledges the distinctiveness of the other.

Aboriginal groups, to use another example, have a unique claim on the land and its resources as the original inhabitants of the country. But just as their treaties cannot be "extinguished" by later legislation, except with their consent, so the rights of other Canadians cannot be extinguished by recognition of aboriginal rights. The task is to find a way to reconcile aboriginal claims with the rights of other Canadians to use common resources and with the duty of the federal government to husband and conserve the environment. On both the Atlantic and Pacific fishing grounds, these issues have exploded. Burnt Church has joined Oka in the annals of Canadian conflict. But we would do well to remember, before we shake our heads at the loss of our civility, that rights don't create the conflict — they merely validate claims. And in the case of disputes over resource management, it is good that claims are understood as rights.[3] We don't want a return to the days when aboriginal peoples had no rights and when the federal government's management of resources went unquestioned. Equally, we don't want people defying the law or taking it into their own hands. If these are the limits of what is tolerable, then courts and legislatures will simply have to find peaceful adjudication somewhere in the middle.[4] Aboriginal peoples and non-aboriginal Canadians cannot live together unless both accept the ultimate sovereignty of Canadian law. Within this common frame, distinctive aboriginal rights can be reconciled with both use rights by other groups and federal environmental controls. The overall objective for all concerned is to find a way to recognize group rights while maintaining the unity of Canadian citizenship, so that we do not have either second-class citizens or privileged ones, and we can maintain equal moral consideration for all Canadians.

This goes beyond balancing rights. It also means balancing acts of recognition. At the moment, the Canadian majority feels that it is faced with multiplying demands for recognition from various minority groups, without these groups accepting any obligation to recognize the majority. This is the heart of the bitterness in English Canada over Quebec. It is the feeling that the Canadian majority is being asked to concede recognition of Quebec's distinct status without earning any commensurate recognition of Canada in return. This perceived inequality of recognition has led many English Canadians to refuse to be party to further concessions. What has proved insupportable is not the nature of Quebec's demands, but the threat of separation that accompanies the demands. Give us what we want or we will go is not a form of recognition but an expression of contempt.

But this inequality in recognition is felt on other fronts of the rights revolution as well. If a sexual minority demands its rights, while at the same time scorning heterosexual family values, it will find it difficult to secure majority recognition. The majority may accept that it cannot impose its values on the minority, but it sees no reason why its values should be ridiculed. Nor does it feel obliged to do more than tolerate minority sexual behaviour. The full approval demanded by minorities is often being met with rituals of political correctness, rather than with a genuine and welcoming change of heart. This will change if recognition becomes genuinely mutual, if both minority and majority agree that in matters sexual, genuine difference of sexual taste is compatible with sub-stantive moral agreement on what is cruel, degrading, coercive, or unfair. What needs to be affirmed, in order to counteract the feeling of moral fragmentation, is actually a commonplace: that shared standards of decency and consent are compatible with a proliferation of sexual practice and experience. In place of a contract of mutual indifference, in which majority and minority sexual cul-tures simply agree to disagree, we need a moral dialogue that allows us to reach agreement on the forms of cruelty, neglect, and abuse that we jointly condemn, and on the forms of committed concern we wish to encourage. Indeed, in a process of mutual recognition on sexual and family matters, the ideal is that both minorities and majorities share experiences and learn from each other, especially in the matter of raising children.

In the field of aboriginal rights, some aboriginal groups demand recognition while speaking of whites as "settler colonials."[5] To speak in this way, as if settlement were merely a form of imperial domination, is to with-hold recognition of the right of the majority to settle and use the land we both share. This neither promotes resolu-tion of aboriginal title, nor adequately represents the view of aboriginal peoples themselves. Throughout centuries of collaboration between newcomers and aboriginal nations, Native peoples have always accepted, with vary-ing degrees of willingness, the fact that being first possessors of the land is not the only source of legiti-macy for its use. Those who came later have acquired legitimacy by their labours; by putting the soil under cultivation; by uncovering its natural resources; by building great cities and linking them together with railways, highways, and now fibre-optic networks and the Internet. To point out the legitimacy of non-aboriginal settlement in Canada is not to make a declaration about anyone's superiority or inferiority, but simply to assert that each has a fair claim to the land, and thus that it must be shared.[6] In the words used by Chief Justice Antonio Lamer in his important judgment recognizing aboriginal title in *Delgamuukw*, "Let's face it: we are all here to stay."[7]

In other words, recognition is a two-way street. National unity, therefore, depends on equality of rights and equality of recognition: minorities recognize majorities; majorities recognize minorities. Both seek shelter under the arch of a law they can trust, since both have had a hand in building it. This could be called a civic nationalist vision of what should hold the country together.[8] Why call it nationalist? Isn't that a dangerous word? I could call it patriotism instead, but that would reproduce an invidious distinction between positive patriotism and negative nationalism. In fact, "patriotism" is simply the name we give to our love of country, while "nationalism" is the epithet we apply to other people's.[9] In fact, there is nothing intrinsically fanatical or extreme about nationalism, if we define it as a principled love of country. Canadians have good reasons to love their country, and I would argue that our rights culture is one of them. As I maintained in my first lecture, the essential distinctiveness of Canada itself lies in the fact that we are a tri-national community, trying to balance individual and collective rights without sacrificing the unity and equality of our citizenship. If you ask me what I love about my country, this is it.

It may seem strange to confess a love for something so seemingly legalistic and desiccated as rights. Yet we need to think of rights as something more than a dry enumeration of entitlements in constitutional codes, as more than a set of instruments that individuals use to defend themselves. Rights create and sustain culture and by culture we mean habits of the heart. Rights create community. They do so because once we believe in equal rights, we are committed to the idea that rights are indivisible. Defending your own rights means being committed to defending the rights of others.

Citizens of at least one Canadian province know a great deal about indivisibility. In 1998, a woman who had been forcibly sterilized as a child in an Alberta institution, on the grounds that she was unfit to raise children, brought suit for compensation against the Alberta government. As many as 500 other women had been treated in this way, and the premier of Alberta, fearing a wave of expensive claims, introduced legislation to curtail the rights of these women to full compensation.[10] This legislation explicitly overrode the women's rights as set out in the Canadian Charter of Rights and Freedoms. Alberta citizens raised a storm of protest that forced the premier to abandon the legislation and pay full compensation not just to the wronged woman, but to all the other women who had been sterilized without consent. When she won her case, the victorious woman told reporters, with a wry chuckle, "Not bad for a moron." And not bad for the thousands of fellow citizens who stood up for her rights.

The commitment to indivisibility goes with a commitment to mutual sacrifice. All rights cost us something. Even when we don't avail ourselves of our entitlements, others do, and we pay for their use.[11] Belonging to a rights community implies that we surrender some portion of our freedom to sustain the collective entitlements that make our life possible. This idea of sacrifice is the very core of what it means to belong to a national community: paying taxes, obeying the law, submitting disputes to adjudication and abiding peacefully by these decisions. Sacrifice does not stop there. The reason that war memorials occupy a central symbolic place in the national life of all nations, even though the wars remembered are now far away in time, is that they represent the sacrifice that all citizens make to keep a community free.

But nationalism is more than this. It is a way of seeing, a way of recognizing fellow citizens as belonging to a shared rights community, and as being entitled to the protection and the care that the national community can provide.

The central issue for Canada, in the wake of the rights revolution, is whether a rights culture is enough to hold the country together, whether it creates a sufficiently robust sense of belonging, and a sufficiently warmhearted kind of mutual recognition, to enable us to solve our differences peacefully. The criticism most often advanced against a civic nationalist vision of national community is that it is too thin. It bases national solidarity on rights equality, but neither rights nor equality make sufficiently deep claims on the loyalties and affections of people to bond them together over time.[12]

This is a very old worry about societies based on rights. When Edmund Burke, the great Anglo-Irish conservative thinker of the late eighteenth century, fulminated against the type of society he saw coming into being with the French Revolution, he warned that the revolutionaries were laying themselves open to continual rebellion.[13] For these new societies were based on contract, on consent, on agreements between parties that could be dissolved. By contrast, the *ancien régime* societies, whose disappearance he lamented, had been based on tradition, history, common origins, and all the deepest sources of human affection and commitment. The enduring relevance of Burke's critique suggests that he identified a crucial weakness in rights-based societies. Clearly, rights are not enough. The elements that hold a country like Canada together run deeper than rights: the land, shared memory, shared opportunity, and shared hope. Yet Burke and his fellow conservatives underestimated the power of rights as a source of legitimacy and cohesion in modern societies, just as they sentimentalized the legitimacy of the *ancien régime*. The ancient and immemorial tissue of connections was insufficient to keep the France of the *ancien régime* together, and the democratic republic that succeeded it, which was based on consent and contract, has endured for two hundred years.

Yet even though contractual societies have shown

themselves to be remarkably robust, we continue to
worry that, to paraphrase William Butler Yeats, the centre
cannot hold. To focus these old anxieties about contract
and consent on contemporary Canada, I want to contrast
civic nationalist states and ethnic nationalist ones. Civic
nationalist states are created by formal constitutional acts
of citizens, much as the French republic was created by
the revolution. Canada, for example, is a civic nationalist
state, and it was formed by a compact of its citizens in
1867. We are, to use Richard Gwyn's useful phrase, a
state-nation, a national community created and held
together by the rights framework, infrastructure, and
services of our government.[14]

An ethnic nationalist state recognizes its citizens on
the basis of common ancestry, language, religion, customs, and rituals. Here shared ancestry — or to use a
more emotional phrase, common blood — forms the basis
of both identity and mutual recognition. Germany could
be described as a national community of language speak-
ers whose identity and ethnicity existed before the
German state. In contrast to Canada, a state-nation, Germany is a nation-state, one in which identity is provided
primarily by common national origins, and secondarily
by common rights and state entitlements.[15]

Let's concede that no nation is ever only ethnic or civic
in the principles of its cohesion. We are talking here of
ideal types.[16] America is held together by both the civic
contract enshrined in its constitution and the fact that a
majority of its population, while striated with a vast
mixture of minorities, remains white, Christian, and

English-speaking. Yet the dominance of this silent majority will soon pass. In the next century, a majority of
Americans will be not be white, Christian, or English-
speaking. Hence the anxiety with which commentators,
most of them from this vanishing majority, ask whether
equality of rights will be enough, in the absence of common origins, to hold the republic together.[17]

Canada faces similar challenges. It is held together not
just by its constitution, but by formidably strong links of
common ancestry. The problem, however, is that our
ancestry is a double, even triple, inheritance. In Quebec,
the majority francophone community traces its ancestry
to the original French settlers, and English Canadians
trace theirs to the Scottish, English, and Irish immigrants
who opened the frontier from the eighteenth century
onward. One million aboriginal Canadians, meanwhile,
trace their ancestry back to the heritage of the tribal
nations of North America. This triple inheritance doesn't
necessarily weaken the country — it may even strengthen
it — but it does mean that the principles of national unity
cannot be found by joint appeal to common origins.

This is essentially why Canada has no choice but to
gamble on rights, to found its unity on civic nationalist
principles. Its unity must be derived from common principles rather than common origins. The importance of
these principles of unity is only redoubled by the impact
of immigration. If there are more than seventy languages
spoken in the homes of only one of our major cities,
Toronto, then it is clear that we need a single common
language to communicate together, and it is also clear

that rights, not roots, are what will hold us together in the future.[18]

The Canadian majority in the next century will be unrecognizably different from the majority I grew up in as a child. Already Canadians of Chinese, Sikh, and Ukrainian origin have occupied the highest offices of state, and more will do so as time goes by. The new Canadian elite has no common origin, only a commitment to common values. But as "new Canadians" make their way to the top, their demands for inclusion are forcing a change in our most basic mythologies. Canadians from these new communities refuse to accept the very concept of Canada as a pact between founding races — that is, the English, the French, and the aboriginal peoples. This concept seems to accord no place to them. Most of them can accept that original inhabitants may have claims to territory and language that are withheld from newcomers. But as these communities grow in number and size, it will be rights delivery, not myths of common origin, that will hold us together. Indeed, without a common fabric of citizenship, without common rights, it is difficult to see what will enable a multicultural society to cohere.[19]

There is no reason why ethnic heterogeneity is incompatible with national unity. The proviso is simply that all Canadians accept and respect each other as rights-bearing equals. We have a long way to go in this regard. That is why, for example, police brutality towards ethnic minorities is — or should be — a national-unity issue, for when servants of the law do not obey the law, when they select particular groups for ill treatment, the very identity of the country as a community of equals is put in question. The proper response to incidents of police brutality in our community is not, as is often argued, more race sensitivity training, but rather is more training in justice, more understanding that the *sine qua non* of unity, civility, and social order is equal protection under the law.

As the rest of Canada moves rapidly towards ethnic heterogeneity and a concept of unity based on shared civic values, Quebec still hesitates over the temptation to pursue a different course, to separate from Canada and seek national sovereignty on the basis of ethnic majority rule. It does so in the face of the exactly the same demographic forces that are changing the face of Toronto. There must be as many languages spoken in the playgrounds of Montreal schools as there are in Toronto or Vancouver. The new Quebec is black, brown, Asian, and white.

Quebec has always been a heterogeneous society, and most people's origins are not exactly *pure laine*, as the happy frequency of entirely francophone O'Neils and O'Briens attests. But a minority current in nationalist opinion thinks of Quebec as the homeland of Quebecers *de vieille souche* (i.e., ancestors of the original inhabitants). Independence is seen primarily as a vehicle to create ethnic majority rule. In moments of crisis and disappointment, such as the defeat of the Quebec referendum in 1995, these nationalists blame defeat on Quebec's minorities, the alien enemy within. Not surprisingly, Quebec's minorities do not believe their rights will be secure in an independent Quebec. They look to Canada, and to its

Charter of Rights and Freedoms, as the ultimate safe-guard of their liberties.

Quebec separatism is undoubtedly an ethnic national-ism, rooted historically in a myth of separate ancestry, but most nationalists aspire to a civic Quebec, capable of incorporating all of its inhabitants. This split between an ethnic heart and a civic conscience is the fundamental contradiction in Quebec nationalist appeal. And the nationalist project is fated to political failure as long as it is unable to persuade the increasingly significant immigrant minorities of the sincerity of its civic and inclusive aspirations.

Separatism is also fated to failure as long as Canada manages to persuade French Canadians to participate in national life. Quebec has never been the only national home of French-speaking Canadians. In reality, as John Ralston Saul has done so much to remind us, Canadian national politics has always been held together by a part-nership between French- and English-speaking leaders. From Baldwin and Lafontaine in the 1840s to King and Lapointe in the 1920s, Québécois leaders have made Canada, and not just Quebec, their home.[20] These partner-ships realized the quintessential Canadian achievements: responsible government, independence from Great Britain, the creation of a national railway, and equality of citizenship. These partnerships endure to this day, and English Canadians, who have been ruled by three French-speaking prime ministers since 1945, do not understand why Québécois feel compelled to seek mas-tery in a small house called Quebec when they already exercise mastery in a larger one called Canada.

There is little doubt that Quebec qualifies as a nation, if by nation we mean a human group who think of themselves as such, speak a common language, and adhere to common myths of origin and common political principles. If Quebecers are a nation, they ought to be able to govern themselves. Yet self-determination does not necessarily imply a right of secession. Secession, with full statehood, is justified when nations are threatened with destruction, when only the possession of state power can guarantee their survival. Kosovars, for example, have a claim to both self-determination and secession, because under Serbian rule, they were subjected to unquestionable oppression. This oppression made it impossible for them to survive in Yugoslavia.[21] But Quebec does not face a challenge to its existence, and Quebecers do not need to have a state of their own in order to rule their own affairs. Most nations, in fact, secure self-determination by sharing the state with other nations, by securing effective self-government within a devolved system of power. And so it has proved in the devolved federal experiment that is Canada.

In the absence of a claim to secession based on clear evidence of oppression, Quebec separatists work up their appeal by alleging that federalism blocks the province's aspirations to full self-determination. Yet the claim seems specious, since anyone with eyes to see realizes that the Quebec government enjoys full power in education, language policy, employment, and immigration. This suggests that the ultimate issue is not the real division of powers within the federal system, but the symbolism of sovereignty. Many Quebecers do not feel they have ever taken full psychological and emotional possession of the federal state, and they look to the creation of their own to feel the final sense of being masters in their own house. If this is the issue, then further constitutional devolution in Canada is a waste of time. Further concessions are beside the point.

The real issue is that we do not share the same vision of our country's history. The problem is not one of rights or powers, but one of truth. We do not inhabit the same historical reality. And it is time we did. For two genera-tions, English Canada has asked, with earnest respect, "What does Quebec want?" It is time for English Canada to say who *we* are and what *our* country is. The answer is: we are a partnership of nations, a community of peoples united in common citizenship and rights. We do possess a common history, and like it or not, we had better begin sharing a common truth.

Here, for example, is the truth as most of English Canada sees it. The British Conquest of 1763, far from extinguishing the French fact in North America, actually brought the Québécois their first experience of self-government. This has been the case since the Quebec Act of 1774, when the British Crown recognized the rights of those of the Catholic religion, the distinctiveness of French law, and the right of *les habitants* to use French as an official language. The result is that for more than two centuries, Quebec has shared the same democratic institutions as the rest of the country, as well as enjoying recognition of its distinctive national character. Indeed, one essential element of Quebec's distinctiveness, in comparison with the American republic to the south, is that its National Assembly follows the norms and traditions of British parliamentary democracy.

The point I am making is that rights will not keep us together if competing visions of historical truth continue to divide us. In the Canadian case, the truths each side holds to be self-evident are the truths that divide us. So how are we to proceed? One way is simply to lay the two truths side by side, acknowledge their incompatibility, and then seek, in so far as it is possible, to put these disagreements to one side. Few societies ever achieve genuinely shared truth between majorities and minorities, however, so let us shed our illusions about securing a unity based on consensus. Yet agreeing to disagree is not enough. We need to narrow the gap between our versions of the truth, always accepting that a gap of some kind will remain. The Conquest will always be the Conquest for Québécois, but we may in time persuade them that this was a conquest like no other, for it ultimately laid the basis for the survival of a democratic Quebec in North America.

Conceding special status for Quebec in constitutional negotiations is probably inevitable, but it does nothing by itself to alter each side's view of the historical truth of Quebec's place in the Canadian confederation. Special status will not redress the Conquest. Nor will it necessarily make Quebecers more willing to accept the English version of the historical record. This means we should cease believing that constitutional settlements can end historical arguments. In reality, they can only produce a new basis for ongoing and unending dialogue.

Truth is truth and rights are rights, and the debate about the proper extent of both will go on. Indeed, it is only when dialogue becomes frozen, when there is no movement, that rupture becomes likely. To commit ourselves to the idea that the search for national unity has no end is not to despair, but merely to acknowledge that it is the very essence of nation-states that they harbour within them incompatible visions of the national story. Holding a nation together does not require us to force these incompatible stories into one, but simply to keep them in dialogue with each other and, if possible, learning from each other. And we have learned. No one in an English-Canadian school today learns the history I did as a child, a history that excluded Native peoples and the Québécois experience of being hewers of wood and drawers of water in their own land.

We need to understand recognition between peoples as something more than a process of concession and negotiation alone. Properly considered, recognition is an act of enlargement that enables both sides to envisage new possibilities of living together. We don't simply recognize each other for what we are; we recognize what we could become together. To do that, we have to recognize what we already are: a peaceable kingdom, a place where languages, cultures, and peoples shelter together under the arch of justice. This is our raison d'être, our example to the world, our never-quite-realized possibility.

These lectures have tried to point out exactly where this Canadian possibility lies. But the lectures have also tried to situate the Canadian experience in a larger context. The revolution has been global, and the challenge it has posed has been to all democratic societies trying to cohere and live justly in an age of rights. The challenge has been to reconcile community with diversity in an age of entitlements. The rights revolution has made us all aware of how different we are, both as individuals and as peoples. Our differences, small as they may seem, are the basis of our identity. Call it the narcissism of minor difference.[22] We don't dwell on what we share; our every fashion statement declares that we are singular.

This doesn't mean we share nothing at all. Isaiah Berlin used to say that our moral language inscribes us within a "human horizon."[23] We disagree about the ultimate ends and purposes of human life, but in the end, we do so within that horizon. Values — to call them human at all — must be within the human horizon. That is why a rights culture is not relativistic: murder, violence, theft, betrayal, and lying are recognizably the same in any culture or historical epoch. But this common human horizon is far away; it is the outer boundary. Closer to home, within this shared horizon, we can have profound disagreements: murder is murder, but is abortion, for example, murder? Irreconcilable moral conflict occurs constantly because even when we start from the same principles, we disagree as to their meaning or application in specific cases. So if we really are that different, how do we ever manage to generate enough agreement to live together in peace?

This is where empathy — the human capacity to enter other people's minds — plays such a constitutive role. We enter other minds not merely because we can, but because we need to. We need other people's approval; our very selves depend on knowing what others think of us. We need others because we are blind to ourselves. As Virginia Woolf said, there is a shilling-sized circle in the middle of the back of our heads that, try as we might, we can never manage to see. Only others can see it for us and tell us what it looks like. Our very individualism is social.

The precondition for order in a liberal society is an act of the imagination: *not* a moral consensus or shared values, but the capacity to understand moral worlds different from our own. We may be different, but we can imagine what it would be like to *be each other*.

Our capacity for empathy is limited. In *Shoah*, Claude Lanzmann's film about the Holocaust in Poland, you will remember the Polish farmer whose fields abutted a death camp. Ash rained down on his fields. He was asked what he felt when he saw fellow human beings going up in smoke. He replied, "I cut my finger, I feel it; when someone else cuts his finger, I only see it."

Imagination carries us only so far; our own sensations are invariably more real to us than the experience of others. We live at the centre of concentric circles of decreasing impingement: first ourselves, then those we love, and only much later, and much more imperfectly, our fellow creatures. But the imperfect moral impingement that others make upon us is as much a fact about us as our selfishness. It is on these facts — and our capacity to imagine them — that we build such community as we can.

How do we generate a world in common? We take actual human individuals — rich, poor, young, old, homosexual, heterosexual, white, black, in between, Catholic, Protestant, Muslim, Jew (i.e., human beings in all their embodied difference) — and we imagine them as equal bearers of rights. Go into any courtroom, police station, or welfare office, and you will find real individuals ignoring the different surfaces of each person they deal with and addressing the juridical equal beneath. They are addressing a moral fiction. Yet it is this fiction, and our devotion to it, that enables us to be just. The entire legitimacy of public institutions depends on our being attentive to difference while treating all as equal. This is the gamble, the unique act of the imagination on which our society rests.

It is a new gamble, conceived in the seventeenth century by the founding fathers of liberal political philosophy, men like John Locke. It could be argued that they never thought a rights community could be composed of literally anyone. Their original thought experiment was confined exclusively to white propertied males. But once this ideal was imagined, the die was cast. No sooner had white propertied males begun to imagine themselves as rights-bearing equals than the propertyless began to ask why they were excluded . . . then women . . . then non-white peoples. Once this type of liberal imagination takes root in a society, it becomes logically untenable to withhold its promise from all humankind.

The political and social history of Western society is the story of the struggle of all human groups to gain inclusion. This vast historical process, which began in the European wars of religion in the sixteenth century, has been brought to a successful conclusion only now, in the rights revolution of the past forty years.

All of this is so much a part of our lived history that we barely notice its enormous historical significance. We are living in the first human society that has actually attempted to create a political community on the assumption that everyone — literally *everyone* — has the right to belong. We are all on the same perilous adventure, whether we live with our differences or die because of them.

From Bosnia to Afghanistan, from Rwanda to Kosovo, ethnic warriors seem bent on proving that rights equality among human beings of different races is a sentimental fiction. In place of societies built on rights, they are hacking out societies whose unity is based in blood and fantasies of common origin. What we are trying to prove, in societies that incorporate all human beings into the same political community, is that the ethnic cleansers are wrong, and that their vision of the future need not come to pass, for us or for the people they tyrannize.

We have reason to be hopeful, and not just because places like Canada are rich and have capacities to conciliate conflict that are denied poorer societies. We are lucky too because, as colonial peoples, we were schooled in the life of liberty. Today, in our multi-ethnic, multicultural cities, we are trying to vindicate a new experiment in ethnic peace, and we have learned that the preconditions of order are simple: equal protection under the law, coupled with the capacity for different peoples to behave towards each other not as members of tribes or clans, but as citizens. We do not require very much in the way of shared values, or even shared lives. People should live where they want, and with whom they want. The key precondition is equality of rights; it all depends whether our differences can shelter under the protecting arch of a legitimate legal order.

So the unity and coherence of a liberal society are not threatened because we come from a thousand different traditions, worship different gods, eat different foods, live in different sections of town, and speak different languages. What is required of us is recognition, empathy, and if possible, reconciliation. To use, once again, the words chosen by a wise French-Canadian judge when he delivered a judgment that brought long-delayed justice to fellow citizens of aboriginal origin, "Let's face it, we're all here to stay."

NOTES

I: The Rights Revolution

1. Tom Wicker, *A Time to Die: The Attica Prison Revolt* (New York: Times Books, 1975).
2. On New Zealand aboriginal claims law and traditions, see F. M. Brookfield, *Waitangi and Indigenous Rights: Revolution Law and Legitimation* (Auckland: Auckland University Press, 1999).
3. Peter H. Russell, *Constitutional Odyssey: Can Canadians Be a Sovereign People?* (Toronto: University of Toronto Press, 1992).
4. "In the Matter of Section 53 of the Supreme Court Act (Reference Re Secession of Quebec), [1998]," S.C.R. 217. See also Diane F. Orentlicher, "Separation Anxiety: International Responses to Ethno-Separatist Claims," *Yale Journal of International Law* 23, no. 1 (1998).
5. J. P. Humphrey, *Human Rights and the United Nations: A Great Adventure* (New York: Transnational, 1984); see also Johannes Morsink, *The Universal Declaration of Human*

Rights: Origins, Drafting and Intent (Philadelphia: University of Pennsylvania Press, 1999).

6. John Packer, "Making International Law Matter in Preventing Ethnic Conflict: A Practitioner's Perspective," *New York University Journal of International Law and Politics* 32 (Spring 2000): 3, 715–24.

7. I discussed the work of Louise Arbour in Kosovo in *Virtual War: Kosovo and Beyond* (Toronto: Penguin, 2000).

8. Will Kymlicka, *Multicultural Citizenship: A Liberal Theory of Minority Rights* (Oxford: Clarendon Press, 1995).

9. James Tully, *Strange Multiplicity: Constitutionalism in an Age of Diversity* (Cambridge: Cambridge University Press, 1995); Charles Taylor, "The Politics of Recognition," in *Multiculturalism: Examining the Politics of Recognition*, ed. Amy Gutmann (Princeton, N.J.: Princeton University Press, 1994); Russell, *Constitutional Odyssey*.

10. Canada, "Equality Rights," in *The Charter of Rights and Freedoms: A Guide for Canadians* (Ottawa: Publications Canada, 1984): "Subsection 1 does not preclude any law, program or activity that has as its object the amelioration of conditions of disadvantaged individuals or groups, including those that are disadvantaged because of race, national or ethnic origin, colour, religion, sex, age or mental or physical disability."

11. Kirk Makin, "Canadian Legal Wisdom a Hot Commodity Abroad," *Globe and Mail*, 1 Sept. 2000.

12. Richard Rorty, *Truth and Moral Progress: Philosophical Papers* (Cambridge: Cambridge University Press, 1998), 11.

13. Joel Bakan, *Just Words: Constitutional Rights and Social Wrongs* (Toronto: University of Toronto Press, 1997), 94–98.

14. On the distinction between "external protections" for

minorities and "internal restrictions" within minority groups, see Kymlicka, *Multicultural Citizenship*, 7.

15. Avishai Margalit and Moshe Halbertal, "Liberalism and the Right to Culture," *Social Research* 61, no. 3: 491–510.

16. Bakan, *Just Words*, introduction.

17. "Judge Refuses to Ban Spanking of Children," *Globe and Mail*, 6 July 2000; "Court Upholds Child Spanking," *National Post*, 6 July 2000.

18. Ronald Beiner, *What's the Matter with Liberalism?* (Berkeley: University of California Press, 1992), ch. 4.

19. I take these points further in my book *Human Rights as Politics and as Idolatry: The Tanner Lectures in Human Values* (Princeton, N.J.: Princeton University Press, 2001).

20. On the idea of deliberation, see Amy Gutmann and Dennis Thompson, *Democracy and Disagreement* (Cambridge, Mass: Belknap Press, 1997).

II: Human Rights and Human Differences

1. The *locus classicus* on rights as bourgeois ideology is to be found in Karl Marx, "On the Jewish Question" (1843). In the Canadian context, the best critique of the incapacity of the Canadian Charter of Rights and Freedoms to focus on social and economic disadvantage is to be found in Bakan, *Just Words*, and in a different vein, in Michael Mandel, *The Charter of Rights and the Legalization of Politics in Canada*, 2d ed. (Toronto: Thompson Educational Publishing, 1994).

2. Bakan, *Just Words.*

3. Leszek Kolakowski, *Modernity on Endless Trial* (Chicago: University of Chicago Press, 1990).

4. Joseph de Maistre, *Considérations sur la France* (1797), ed. P. Manent (Paris: Éditions Complexe, 1988), 87; see also

Antonio Cassese, "Are Human Rights Truly Universal?" in *The Politics of Human Rights,* ed. Obrad Savic (London: Verso, 1999), 120–49. On de Maistre generally, see Isaiah Berlin, *The Crooked Timber of Humanity: Chapters in the History of Ideas,* ed. Henry Hardy (London: John Murray, 1990).

5. Jeremy Bentham, "Anarchical Fallacies," in *The Works of Jeremy Bentham,* ed. John Bowring (Edinburgh, 1843), 494–501.

6. I have written extensively about the interaction between globalized media and human-rights consciousness. See, for example, *The Warrior's Honour: Ethnic War and the Modern Conscience* (Toronto: Penguin, 1998).

7. Kymlicka, *Multicultural Citizenship,* 124–27.

8. On the ethics of immigration restriction, see Michael Walzer, *Spheres of Justice* (Oxford: Martin Robertson, 1983), 40–46; see also J. H. Carens, "Aliens and Citizens: The Case for Open Borders," *Review of Politics* 49(2): 251–273.

9. Heather Pringle, "Alberta Barren," *Saturday Night* (June 1997): 30–37; *Muir v. Alberta,* 305, 36, *Alberta Law Reports* 3d.: 305–73.

10. Charles Dickens, *Bleak House* (New York: W.W. Norton, 1977), 34–45.

11. One exemplary examination of human equality in our culture is to be found in Shakespeare's *King Lear,* especially the famous speech that begins, "Oh reason not the need," at the end of act 1. Here the king defends the claim that to treat people with respect for their humanity is to treat them differently, each according to his need, for the raiment and retinue fit for a king. I examine this speech in detail in my book *The Needs of Strangers* (Toronto: Penguin, 1984).

12. The most complete discussion of this point is to be found in Primo Levi, *If This Is a Man* (London: Abacus, 1971, 1996).

13. Hannah Arendt, *The Origins of Totalitarianism* (New York: Harcourt and Brace, 1973), 300.

14. On natural rights theories, see Richard Tuck, *Natural Rights Theories* (Cambridge: Cambridge University Press, 1979).

15. A. H. Robertson and J. G. Merrills, *Human Rights in the World*, 4th ed. (Manchester: Manchester University Press, 1996), chs. 4 and 5.

16. Amnesty International, *Rights for All: Country Report, USA* (London: Amnesty International, 1998).

17. For rights narcissism, see Michael Ignatieff, "Out of Order," *Index on Censorship* 3: 98; see also William Schabas, *The Abolition of the Death Penalty in International Law* (Cambridge: Cambridge University Press, 1997).

18. On Eleanor Roosevelt's role in the drafting of the Universal Declaration of Human Rights, and on the evolution of American official attitudes towards international human rights, see Paul Gordon Lauren, *The Evolution of International Human Rights* (Philadelphia: University of Pennsylvania Press, 1998).

19. I discussed the conflict between the right of intervention and rights of popular sovereignty in *Human Rights as Politics and as Idolatry*. See also the useful essays in Mortimer Sellers, ed., *The New World Order: Sovereignty, Human Rights and the Self-Determination of Peoples* (Washington, D.C.: Berg, 1996).

20. This discussion of the criteria for just military intervention owes much to discussions of the International Commission on Kosovo, co-chaired by Richard Goldstone and

Carl Tham, and to the work of commission members Martha Minow, Richard Falk, and Jacques Rupnik. The report is due to be submitted to the secretary-general of the United Nations in New York in October 2000.

21. My own opinion on the morality and legality of the Kosovo intervention is to be found in *Virtual War*.

III: The Pool Table or the Patchwork Quilt: Individual and Group Rights

1. The entire discussion in this chapter is drawn from Tully, *Strange Multiplicity*.

2. Eugen Weber, *Peasants into Frenchmen: The Modernization of Rural France, 1870–1914* (Stanford, Calif.: Stanford University Press, 1979).

3. For one example of this historical tenacity, see Joseph Gosnell, "Making History: Chief Gosnell's Historic Speech to the British Columbia Legislature," 2 Dec. 1998, on the Nisga'a Treaty. Available online at www.ntc.bc.ca. See also Augie Fleras and Jean Leonard Elliott, *The "Nations Within": Aboriginal-State Relations in Canada, the United States and New Zealand* (Toronto: Oxford University Press, 1992). On aboriginal rights to self-determination, see Garth Nettheim, "'Peoples' and 'Populations': Indigenous Peoples and the Rights of Peoples," in *The Rights of Peoples,* ed. James Crawford (Oxford: Clarendon Press, 1988); also Patrick Thornberry, *International Law and the Rights of Minorities* (Oxford: Clarendon Press, 1991), 331–75.

4. Pierre E. Trudeau, *Federalism and the French Canadians* (Toronto: Macmillan, 1968). See also Canada, Prime Minister's Office, *Federalism for the Future: A Statement of Policy by the Government of Canada* (Ottawa: Queen's Printer, 1968).

5. Canada, Department of Indian Affairs and Northern Development, *Statement of the Government of Canada on Indian Policy* (Ottawa: Indian Affairs, 1969).

6. "Dhaliwal Offers Fishing Deals to BC Natives to Avoid Litigation," *National Post*, 8 Apr. 2000.

7. The Musqueam band in Vancouver has been sued in Canadian federal court in a dispute with non-aboriginal homeowners over property taxes on Musqueam reserve lands. See *Huyck et al. versus Musqueam Indian Band Council*, Federal Court, Vancouver, May 2000.

8. Quebec, La Charte de la langue française, title 1, chapter 8, sections 72–85. Available online at www.olf.gouv.qc.ca.

9. I am indebted to Will Kymlicka's discussion of state neutrality in *Multicultural Citizenship*, 114–15.

10. For a critique of multiculturalist politics in Canada, see Neil Bissoondath, *Selling Illusions: The Cult of Multiculturalism in Canada* (Toronto: Penguin Books, 1994). On multiculturalism in the United States, see David Hollinger, *Post-Ethnic America: Beyond Multiculturalism* (New York: Basic Books, 1995).

11. Marc Chevrier, "Laws and Language in Quebec: The Principles and Means of Quebec's Language Policy" (Quebec: Ministry of International Relations, 1997). Available online at www.mri.gouv.qc.ca.

12. See Kymlicka, *Multicultural Citizenship*, 163–72.

13. Margalit and Halbertal, "Liberalism and the Right to Culture."

14. Martha Minow, *Between Vengeance and Forgiveness: Facing History after Genocide and Mass Violence* (Boston: Beacon Press, 1998). Also Eleazar Barkan, *The Guilt of Nations: Restitution and Negotiating Historical Injustices* (New York: W.W. Norton, 2000).

15. Charles E. Hendry, *Beyond Traplines: Does the Church Really Care? Towards an Assessment of the Work of the Anglican Church of Canada with Canada's Native Peoples* (Toronto: Anglican Book Centre, 1998); "Money Could Run Out in 2001," *Anglican Journal* 126, no. 6 (June 2000). See also, "Priests Ask Taxpayers to Cover Cost of Abuses," *Globe and Mail*, 12 July 2000.

16. I am indebted to the magisterial summary of these events in Russell, *Constitutional Odyssey*, chs. 7–10.

17. For a narrative of the constitutional journey of Canada from a sovereigntist perspective, see www.premier.gouv. qc.ca/premier_ministre.

18. Canada, "Report of the Royal Commission on Aboriginal Peoples," vol. 2 (Ottawa: Canada Communications Group, 1996), 163–244. See also *Delgamuukw v. the Queen et al.*, Supreme Court of British Columbia, 0843 (1991).

19. Canada, Department of Indian and Northern Affairs, *Aboriginal Self-Government: Federal Policy Guide*. Available online at www.inac.gc.ca.

20. Tom Flanagan, *First Nations, Second Thoughts?* (Montreal: McGill-Queen's University Press, 2000), ch. 6.

21. British Columbia Treaty Commission, *Annual Report 2000*. Available online at www.bctreaty.net.

IV: Rights, Intimacy, and Family Life

1. Mary McCarthy and Joanna Radbord, "Family Law for Same-Sex Couples: Chart(er)ing the Course," *Canadian Journal of Family Law* 15, no. 101 (1998).

2. Taylor, "The Politics of Recognition," in *Multiculturalism*, ed. Gutmann.

3. Michael Walzer, *On Toleration* (New Haven, Conn.: Yale

University Press, 1997).

4. Francis Fukuyama, *The Great Disruption: Human Nature and the Reconstitution of Social Order* (New York: The Free Press, 1999). See also Roderick Phillips, *Putting Asunder: A History of Divorce in Western Society* (Cambridge: Cambridge University Press, 1988).

5. George Grant, *English-Speaking Justice* (Toronto: Anansi, 1974, 1985), 69–90.

6. Joseph Schumpeter, *Capitalism, Socialism, and Democracy* (New York: Harper & Brothers, 1942).

7. Christopher Lasch, *Haven in a Heartless World* (New York: Basic Books, 1977); see also Fukuyama, *The Great Disruption.*

8. Nicholas Bala, "A Report from Canada's Gender War Zone: Reforming the Child-Related Provisions of the Divorce Act," *Canadian Journal of Family Law* 16, no. 2 (1999): 163–227.

9. Fukuyama, *The Great Disruption,* 41–42, 84, 115.

10. Winifred Holland, "Intimate Relationships in the New Millennium: The Assimilation of Marriage and Cohabitation," *Canadian Journal of Family Law* 17, no. 1 (2000): 114–68.

11. "Judge Refuses to Ban Spanking of Children," *Globe and Mail,* 6 July 2000.

12. Statistics Canada, *Household Unpaid Work* (Ottawa, 1995).

13. Lionel Trilling, *Sincerity and Authenticity* (Cambridge, Mass.: Harvard University Press, 1972); see also Marshall Berman, *The Politics of Authenticity* (New York: Atheneum, 1970).

14. Fukuyama, *The Great Disruption* (New York: The Free Press, 1999).

15. Teresa Foley, "Dobson v. Dobson: Tort Liability for

Expectant Mothers," *Saskatchewan Law Review* (1998): 61, 177; see also Sandra Rogers, "Case Comment and Note: Winnipeg Child and Family Services v. D.F.G: Juridical Interference with Pregnant Women in the Alleged Interest of the Fetus," *Alberta Law Review* 36, no. 711 (1998).

16. Statistics Canada, *Divorces 1995* (Ottawa, 1995), table 8 at 20. See also Bala, "Canada's Gender War Zone," note 1.

17. Bala, note 1.

18. Bala, note 1.

19. I first made these arguments in a lecture titled "Liberal Values, a Defence: The Keith Davey Lecture," delivered at Victoria College, University of Toronto, 1996.

20. Isaiah Berlin, *Four Essays on Liberty* (New York: Oxford University Press, 1969), 167–72.

V: Rights, Recognition, and Nationalism

1. Richard Gwyn, *Nationalism without Walls: The Unbearable Lightness of Being Canadian* (Toronto: McClelland and Stewart, 1996), ch. 10.

2. Al Etmanski, *A Good Life* (Burnaby, B.C.: Planned Lifetime Advocacy Network, 2000). I am indebted to Vancouver city councillor Sam Sullivan for discussing issues relating to the rights of the disabled with me.

3. "Legal Lobster War Heats Up," *Globe and Mail*, 18 Aug. 2000.

4. "Uneasy Peace Reigns over Burnt Church," *Globe and Mail*, 16 Aug. 2000.

5. Ovide Mercredi and Mary Ellen Turpel, *In the Rapids: Navigating the Future of First Nations* (Toronto: Viking, 1993).

6. Flanagan, *First Nations, Second Thoughts*, ch. 2.

7. Canada, Supreme Court, *Delgamuukw: Decision on Aborigi-*

    nal Title (Vancouver: Greystone Books, 1998), 13.

8. For a discussion of these terms, see my book *Blood and Belonging: Journeys into the New Nationalism* (Toronto: Penguin, 1993), introduction.

9. Maurizio Viroli, *For Love of Country: An Essay on Patriotism and Nationalism* (Oxford: Clarendon Press, 1995).

10. Pringle, "Alberta Barren," 30–37; Graham Thomson, "Outrageous System Regarded Them as Morons," *Edmonton Journal*, 2 Nov. 1999; Muir v. Alberta, 305, 36, *Alberta Law Reports* 3d.: 305–73.

11. Stephen Holmes and Cass R. Sunstein, *The Cost of Rights: Why Liberty Depends on Taxes* (New York: W.W. Norton, 1999).

12. Bernard Yack, "The Myth of the Civic Nation," in *Theorizing Nationalism*, ed. Robert Beiner (Albany: State University of New York Press, 1999), 103–19. Philip Resnick, "Civic and Ethnic Nationalism: Lessons from the Canadian Case," in *Canadian Political Philosophy: Contemporary Reflections*, eds. R. Beiner and W. Norman (Toronto: University of Toronto Press, 2000).

13. Edmund Burke [1790], *Reflections on the Revolution in France* (New York: Oxford University Press, 1993).

14. Gwyn, *Nationalism without Walls*, 255–56.

15. Rogers Brubaker, *Citizenship and Nationhood in France and Germany* (Cambridge, Mass.: Harvard University Press, 1992).

16. Will Kymlicka, "Misunderstanding Nationalism," in *Theorizing Nationalism*, ed. Beiner, 131–41.

17. Arthur Schlesinger, *The Disuniting of America* (New York: Norton, 1992).

18. "Schools Fear for Immigrant Students," *Globe and Mail*, 3 Mar. 1998.

19. Bissoondath, *Selling Illusions*.

20. John Ralston Saul, *Reflections of a Siamese Twin: Canada at the End of the 20th Century* (Toronto: Viking, 1997), chs. 2 and 3.

21. Richard Goldstone and Carl Tham, *International Independent Commission on Kosovo: Final Report* (New York: Oxford University Press, 2000). I was a member of this commission, and I supported the Kosovar claim to conditional independence under international supervision.

22. I used this term in *The Warrior's Honour: Ethnic War and the Modern Conscience* (Toronto: Penguin, 1998).

23. See my book *Isaiah Berlin: A Life* (Toronto: Penguin, 1998).

BIBLIOGRAPHY

Bakan, Joel. *Just Words: Constitutional Rights and Social Wrongs*. Toronto: University of Toronto Press, 1997.

Bala, Nicholas. "A Report from Canada's Gender War Zone: Reforming the Child-Related Provisions of the Divorce Act." *Canadian Journal of Family Law* 16 (163).

Barsh, Russel Lawrence, and James Youngblood Henderson. "Aboriginal Rights, Treaty Rights and Human Rights: Indian Tribes and 'Constitutional Renewal.'" *Journal of Canadian Studies* 17 (2): 55–81.

Beiner, Ronald. *What's the Matter with Liberalism?* Berkeley: University of California Press, 1992.

Borovoy, Alan. "How Not to Fight Racial Hatred." In *Freedom of Expression and the Charter*, edited by David Schneiderman. Toronto: Thomson Publishing, 1991.

British Columbia Treaty Commission. *Annual Report, 2000*. Vancouver, 2000.

Brownlie, Ian. "The Rights of Peoples in International Law." In *The Rights of Peoples*, edited by James Crawford. Oxford: Clarendon Press, 1988.

Canada. *The Charter of Rights and Freedoms: A Guide for*

Canadians. Ottawa: Publications Canada, 1984.

——. "Report of the Royal Commission on Aboriginal Peoples." 5 vols. Ottawa: Canada Communication Group, 1996.

——. Department of Indian and Northern Affairs. *Federal Policy Guide: Aboriginal Self Government.* Ottawa, 1995.

——. Supreme Court. *Delgamuukw: Decision on Aboriginal Title.* Vancouver: Greystone Books, 1998.

——. Supreme Court. Ford v. Quebec (Attorney General). *Dominion Law Reports* 54 (4): 577–636.

Carens, J. H. "Aliens and Citizens: The Case for Open Borders." *Review of Politics* 49 (2): 251–73.

——. "Cosmopolitanism, Nationalism and Immigration: False Dichotomies and Shifting Presumptions." In *Canadian Political Philosophy: Contemporary Reflections,* edited by R. Beiner and W. Norman. Toronto: University of Toronto Press, 2000.

Cassese, Antonio. "Are Human Rights Truly Universal?" In *The Politics of Human Rights,* edited by Obrad Savic. London: Verso, 1999.

Chevrier, Marc. "Laws and Language in Quebec: The Principles and Means of Quebec's Language Policy." Quebec: Ministry of International Relations, February 1997.

Cotler, Irwin. "Racist Incitement: Giving Free Speech a Bad Name." In *Freedom of Expression and the Charter. See* Borovoy.

Eisenberg, Avigail. "The Politics of Individual and Group Difference in Canadian Jurisprudence." *Canadian Journal of Political Science* 27 (March 1994): 3–21.

Etmanski, Al. *A Good Life.* Burnaby, B.C.: Planned Lifetime Advocacy Network, 2000.

Evans, Patricia M., and Gerda Wekerle, eds. *Women and the Canadian Welfare State: Challenges and Change.* Toronto: University of Toronto Press, 1997.

Fleras, Augie, and Jean Leonard Elliott. *The "Nations Within": Aboriginal-State Relations in Canada, the United States and New Zealand*. Toronto: Oxford University Press, 1992.

Gibbins, Roger, and Guy Laforest, eds. *Beyond the Impasse: Toward Reconciliation*. Montreal: Institute for Research on Public Policy, 1998.

Glendon, Mary Ann. *Rights Talk: The Impoverishment of Political Discourse*. New York, The Free Press, 1991.

Gosnell, Joseph. "Making History: Chief Gosnell's Historic Speech to the British Columbia Legislature," 2 Dec. 1998, Victoria, B.C.

Gutmann, Amy, and Dennis Thompson. *Democracy and Disagreement*. Cambridge, Mass.: Belknap Press, 1997.

Gwyn, Richard. *Nationalism without Walls: The Unbearable Lightness of Being Canadian*. Toronto: McClelland and Stewart, 1995.

Hendry, Charles E. *Beyond Traplines: Does the Church Really Care? Towards an Assessment of the Work of the Anglican Church of Canada with Canada's Native Peoples*. Toronto: Anglican Book Centre, 1998.

Hesse, Carla, and Robert Post. *Human Rights in Political Transitions: Gettysburg to Bosnia*. New York: Zone Books, 1999.

Holland, Winifred. "Intimate Relationships in the New Millennium: The Assimilation of Marriage and Cohabitation?" *Canadian Journal of Family Law* 17 (114).

Ignatieff, Michael. *Blood and Belonging: Journeys into the New Nationalism*. Toronto: Penguin, 1993.

——. *Human Rights as Politics and as Idolatry*. Princeton: Princeton University Press, 2001.

——. *Virtual War: Kosovo and Beyond*. Toronto: Penguin, 2000.

——. *The Warrior's Honour: Ethnic War and the Modern Conscience*. Toronto: Penguin, 1998.

Knopf, Rainer, and F. L. Morton, eds. *Charter Politics*. Scarborough, Ont.: Nelson Canada, 1992.

Kymlicka, Will. *Finding Our Way: Rethinking Ethnocultural Relations in Canada*. Toronto: University of Toronto Press, 1998.

———. *Multicultural Citizenship: A Liberal Theory of Minority Rights*. Oxford: Clarendon Press, 1995.

L'Heureux-Dubé, Claire. "Making Equality Work in Family Law." *Canadian Journal of Family Law* 14 (103).

Mandel, Michael. *The Charter of Rights and the Legalization of Politics in Canada*. 2d ed. Toronto: Thompson Educational Publishers, 1994.

McCarthy, Mary, and Joanna L. Radbord. "Family Law for Same-Sex Couples: Chart(er)ing the Course." *Canadian Journal of Family Law* 15 (101).

Mendes, Errol P. "Two Solitudes: Freedom of Expression and Collective Linguistic Rights in Canada: A Case Study of the Ford Decision." *National Journal of Constitutional Law* 1: 283–313.

Moore, Margaret. "Liberal Nationalism and Multiculturalism." In *Canadian Political Philosophy. See* Cairns.

Rae, Bob. *From Protest to Power: Personal Reflections on a Life in Politics*. Toronto: Viking, 1996.

Resnick, Philip. "Civic and Ethnic Nationalism: Lessons from the Canadian Case." In *Canadian Political Philosophy. See* Carens.

Robertson, A. H., and J. G. Merrills. *Human Rights in the World*. 4th ed. Manchester: Manchester University Press, 1996.

Russell, Peter H. *Constitutional Odyssey: Can Canadians Be a Sovereign People?* Toronto: University of Toronto Press, 1992.

Saul, John Ralston. *Reflections of a Siamese Twin: Canada at the End of the 20th Century*. Toronto: Viking, 1997.

Schneiderman, David, and Kate Sutherland, eds. *Charting*

the Consequences: The Impact of Charter Rights on Canadian Law and Politics.* Toronto: University of Toronto
Press, 1997.

Sellers, Mortimer. *The New World Order: Sovereignty,
Human Rights and the Self-Determination of Peoples.*
Washington, D.C.: Berg, 1996.

Sniderman, Paul, Joseph F. Fletcher, Peter H. Russell, and
Philip E. Tetlock. *The Class of Rights: Liberty, Equality and
Legitimacy in Pluralist Democracy.* New Haven: Yale Uni-
versity Press, 1997.

Steiner, Henry J., and Philip Alston. *International Human
Rights in Context: Law, Politics, Morals.* Oxford: Clarendon Press, 1996.

Taylor, Charles. "The Conditions of an Unforced Consensus on Human Rights." In *The Politics of Human Rights.*
See Cassese.

———. "The Politics of Recognition." In *Multiculturalism:
Examining the Politics of Recognition,* edited by Amy
Gutmann. Princeton, N.J.: Princeton University Press,
1994.

Thornberry, Patrick. *International Law and the Rights of
Minorities.* Oxford: Clarendon Press, 1991.

Tully, James. *Strange Multiplicity: Constitutionalism in an
Age of Diversity.* Cambridge: Cambridge University
Press, 1995.

Vetterling-Braggin, Mary, Frederick A. Elliston, and Jane
English, eds. *Feminism and Philosophy.* Totowa, N.J.:
Rowman and Littlefield, 1981.

Waldron, Jeremy. "Minority Cultures and the Cosmopoli-
tan Alternative." In *The Rights of Minority Cultures,*
edited by Will Kymlicka. Toronto: Oxford University
Press, 1995.

Weinrib, Lorraine. "The Activist Constitution." *Policy
Options* (Institute for Research in Public Policy), April
1999.

———. "Does Money Talk? Commercial Expression in the Canadian Constitutional Context." In *Freedom of Expression and the Charter. See* Borovoy.

———. "The Notwithstanding Clause, or the Loophole Cementing the Charter." *Cité Libre* (Oct.–Nov. 1998).

Yack, Bernard. "The Myth of the Civic Nation." In *Theorizing Nationalism*, edited by Robert Beiner. Albany: State University of New York Press, 1999.

INDEX

The CBC Massey Lectures Series

Also available from House of Anansi Press in this prestigious series: